Y0-CDQ-391

FrontPage 2003: Basic

Student Manual

THOMSON
™
COURSE TECHNOLOGY

Australia • Canada • Mexico • Singapore
Spain • United Kingdom • United States

FrontPage 2003: Basic

VP and GM of Courseware:	Michael Springer
Series Product Managers:	Charles G. Blum and Adam A. Wilcox
Developmental Editor:	Brandon Heffernan
Copyeditor:	Ken Maher
Keytester:	Bill Bateman
Series Designer:	Adam A. Wilcox
Cover Designer:	Abby Scholz

For more information contact:

Course Technology
25 Thomson Place
Boston, MA 02210

Or find us on the Web at: www.course.com

For permission to use material from this text or product, submit a request online at: www.thomsonrights.com

Any additional questions about permissions can be submitted by e-mail to: thomsonrights@thomson.com

Trademarks

Disclaimer

ISBNs

    1-4239-1359-0 = Student Manual

    1-4239-1361-2= Student Manual with data CD and CBT

Printed in the United States of America

1 2 3 4 5 6 7 8 9 PM 08 07 06

Contents

Introduction

After reading this introduction, you'll know how to:

A Use Course Technology ILT manuals in general.

B Use prerequisites, a target student description, course objectives, and a skills inventory to set your expectations properly for the course.

C Re-key this course after class.

Topic A: About the manual

Course Technology ILT philosophy

Course Technology ILT manuals facilitate your learning by providing structured interaction with the software itself. While we provide text to explain difficult concepts, the hands-on activities are the focus of our courses. By paying close attention as your instructor leads you through these activities, you'll learn the skills and concepts effectively.

We believe strongly in the instructor-led classroom. During class, focus on your instructor. Our manuals are designed and written to facilitate your interaction with your instructor and not to call attention to the manuals themselves.

We believe in the basic approach of setting expectations, delivering instruction, and providing summary and review afterwards. For this reason, lessons begin with objectives and end with summaries. We also provide overall course objectives and a course summary to provide both an introduction to and a closure on the entire course.

Manual components

The manuals contain these major components:

- Table of contents
- Introduction
- Units
- Course summary
- Quick reference
- Glossary
- Index

Each element is described below.

Table of contents

The table of contents acts as a learning roadmap.

Introduction

The introduction contains information about our training philosophy and our manual components, features, and conventions. It contains target student, prerequisite, objective, and setup information for the specific course.

Units

Units are the largest structural component of the course content. A unit begins with a title page that lists objectives for each major subdivision, or topic, within the unit. Within each topic, conceptual and explanatory information alternates with hands-on activities. Units conclude with a summary comprising one paragraph for each topic, and an independent practice activity that gives you an opportunity to practice the skills you've learned.

The conceptual information takes the form of text paragraphs, exhibits, lists, and tables. The activities are structured in two columns, one telling you what to do, the other providing explanations, descriptions, and graphics.

Course summary

This section provides a text summary of the entire course. It's useful for providing closure at the end of the course. The course summary also indicates the next course in this series, if there is one, and lists additional resources you might find useful as you continue to learn about the software.

Quick reference

The quick reference is an at-a-glance job aid summarizing some of the more common features of the software.

Glossary

The glossary provides definitions for all of the key terms used in this course.

Index

The index at the end of this manual makes it easy for you to find information about a particular software component, feature, or concept.

Manual conventions

We've tried to keep the number of elements and the types of formatting to a minimum in the manuals. This approach aids in clarity and makes the manuals more classically elegant. But there are some conventions and icons you should know about.

Convention	Description
Italic text	In conceptual text, indicates a new term or feature.
Bold text	In unit summaries, indicates a key term or concept. In an independent practice activity, indicates an explicit item that you select, choose, or type.
`Code font`	Indicates code or syntax.

`Longer strings of ►`
`   code will look ►`
`   like this.`
	In the hands-on activities, any code that's too long to fit on a single line is divided into segments by one or more continuation characters (►). This code should be entered as a continuous string of text.

Select **bold item**	In the left column of hands-on activities, bold sans-serif text indicates an explicit item that you select, choose, or type.
Keycaps like (↵ ENTER)	Indicate a key on the keyboard you must press.

Hands-on activities

The hands-on activities are the most important parts of our manuals. They are divided into two primary columns. The "Here's how" column gives short instructions to you about what to do. The "Here's why" column provides explanations, graphics, and clarifications. Here's a sample:

Do it!

A-1:   Creating a commission formula

Here's how	Here's why
1 Open Sales	This is an oversimplified sales compensation worksheet. It shows sales totals, commissions, and incentives for five sales reps.
2 Observe the contents of cell F4	F4 ▼ = =E4*C_Rate
	The commission rate formulas use the name "C_Rate" instead of a value for the commission rate.

For these activities, we've provided a collection of data files designed to help you learn each skill in a real-world business context. As you work through the activities, you'll modify and update these files. Of course, you might make a mistake and, therefore, want to re-key the activity starting from scratch. To make it easy to start over, you'll rename each data file at the end of the first activity in which the file is modified. Our convention for renaming files is to add the word "My" to the beginning of the file name. In the above activity, for example, a file called "Sales" is being used for the first time. At the end of this activity, you would save the file as "My sales," thus leaving the "Sales" file unchanged. If you make a mistake, you can start over using the original "Sales" file.

In some activities, however, it may not be practical to rename the data file. If you want to retry one of these activities, ask your instructor for a fresh copy of the original data file.

Topic B: Setting your expectations

Properly setting your expectations is essential to your success. This topic will help you do that by providing:

- Prerequisites for this course
- A description of the target student at whom the course is aimed
- A list of the objectives for the course
- A skills assessment for the course

Course prerequisites

Before taking this course, you should be familiar with personal computers and the use of a keyboard and a mouse. Furthermore, this course assumes that you've completed the following courses or have equivalent experience:

- *Windows 2000: Basic* or *Windows XP: Basic*
- *Internet Explorer 5.0: Basic*

Target student

The target student for this course should be familiar with personal computers, having experience with Microsoft Windows 2000 or later and Internet Explorer 5.0. You'll get most out of this course if your goal is to become proficient at building Web sites quickly.

Course objectives

These overall course objectives will give you an idea about what to expect from the course. It's also possible that they'll help you see that this course isn't the right one for you. If you think you either lack the prerequisite knowledge or already know most of the subject matter to be covered, you should let your instructor know that you think you're misplaced in the class.

After completing this course, you will know how to:

- Identify important features and components of the FrontPage environment.
- Create, and format a Web page, create bulleted, numbered, multilevel, and definition lists, check spelling throughout a Web site, and use Find and Replace.
- Create and test hyperlinks, create a navigation structure, add and test a navigation bar, and update hyperlinks.
- Insert and edit images, create and modify a photo gallery, create image links, and add hotspots to an image.

- Insert a table, add images and text, delete and insert rows and columns, insert a nested table, add captions, and format tables.

- Set page properties, add and remove background images, apply a theme to a Web site, and customize a theme.

- View the HTML tree structure and manipulate items by using the Quick Tag Selector, edit tags by using the Quick Tag Editor, use the IntelliSense feature, set word wrap and line numbers, customize code indentation, find matching tags, insert comments, create bookmarks, create and insert code snippets, and optimize HTML code.

- Publish a Web site to the World Wide Web, LAN, or SharePoint Portal Server, and set permissions for a Web site.

Skills inventory

Use the following form to gauge your skill level entering the class. For each skill listed, rate your familiarity from 1 to 5, with five being the most familiar. *This is not a test.* Rather, it's intended to provide you with an idea of where you're starting at the beginning of class. If you're wholly unfamiliar with all the skills, you might not be ready for the class. If you think you already understand all of the skills, you might need to move on to the next course in the series. In either case, you should let your instructor know as soon as possible.

Skill	1	2	3	4	5
Navigating through FrontPage views					
Creating a new blank Web page					
Entering and formatting text on a Web page					
Creating bulleted, numbered, and multilevel lists					
Checking spelling throughout a Web site					
Using Find and Replace					
Creating and testing hyperlinks					
Linking to a page on the Internet and to an e-mail address					
Creating a navigation structure					
Adding and testing navigation bars					
Testing and updating hyperlinks					
Inserting and modifying images					
Adding images to a list					
Creating and modifying a photo gallery					
Using images as hyperlinks					
Adding a hotspot to an image					
Inserting tables					
Drawing a table					
Inserting a nested table					
Adding a caption to a table					
Copying content from one cell to multiple cells					

Skill	1	2	3	4	5
Modifying table and cell properties					
AutoFormatting a table					
Setting page properties					
Applying a theme to a Web page					
Customizing a theme					
Viewing the HTML tree structure					
Using the Quick Tag Selector					
Editing tags					
Using the IntelliSense feature					
Creating and inserting code snippets					
Optimizing HTML code					
Publishing a Web site					
Publishing a Web site to the SharePoint Portal sever					
Setting permissions for a Web site					

Topic C: Re-keying the course

If you have the proper hardware and software, you can re-key this course after class. This section explains what you need in order to do so and how to do it.

Computer requirements

To re-key this course, your personal computer must have:

- A keyboard and a mouse
- Pentium 233 MHz processor (or higher)
- 128 MB RAM
- 400 MB of available hard drive space
- A CD-ROM drive
- An SVGA monitor (800×600 minimum resolution support)
- Internet access, for the following purposes:
  - Installing the latest service packs and security patches from www.windowsupdate.com
  - Activating the FrontPage software
  - Downloading and installing Macromedia Flash Player
  - Downloading the Student Data files from www.courseilt.com (if necessary)

Setup instructions to re-key the course

Before you re-key the course, you need to perform the following steps.

1 Install Microsoft Windows 2000 Professional on an NTFS partition according to the software manufacturer's instructions. Then, install the latest critical updates and service packs from www.windowsupdate.com. (You can also use Windows XP Professional, although the screen shots in this course were taken using Windows 2000, so your screens might look somewhat different.)

2 Adjust your computer's display properties as follows:

   a Open the Control Panel and double-click Display to open the Display Properties dialog box.

   b On the Settings tab, change the Colors setting to True Color (24 bit) and the Screen area to 800 by 600 pixels.

   c On the Appearance tab, set the Scheme to Windows Classic.

   d Click OK. If you are prompted to accept the new settings, click OK and click Yes. Then, if necessary, close the Display Properties dialog box.

3 Install the Internet Information Services (IIS) add-on, as follows:

   a Run the Microsoft Windows 2000 Professional CD.

   b Click Install Add-On Components.

   c In the Windows Components Wizard dialog box, in the components list, check Internet Information Services (IIS).

   d Click Next.

4   Adjust the computer's Internet settings as follows:

    a   On the desktop, right-click the Internet Explorer icon and choose Properties to open the Internet Properties dialog box.

    b   On the Connections tab, click Setup to start the Internet Connection Wizard.

    c   Click Cancel. A message box will appear.

    d   Check "Do not show the Internet Connection wizard in the future," and click Yes.

    e   Re-open the Internet Properties dialog box.

    f   On the General tab, click Use Blank, click Apply, and click OK.

5   Install Microsoft FrontPage 2003.

    a   When prompted for the CD Key, enter the 25-character code included with your software.

    b   Under Choose an install type, select Complete, and then click Next.

    c   After installation is complete, restart the computer.

6   Install the latest version of Macromedia Flash Player.

    a   Go to http://www.macromedia.com/downloads.

    b   Click the link for Macromedia Flash Player.

    c   Follow the on-screen instructions to download and install the player.

7   Configure Windows Explorer to display file extensions.

    a   Start Windows Explorer.

    b   Choose Tools, Folder Options.

    c   Activate the View tab.

    d   Under Advanced settings, clear "Hide file extensions for known file types."

    e   Click OK.

    f   Close Windows Explorer.

8   Start FrontPage. If the Microsoft Office FrontPage 2003 Activation Wizard appears, click Cancel.

9   Turn off the Office Assistant as follows:

    a   If the Office Assistant is not displayed, choose Help, Show the Office Assistant.

    b   Right-click the Office Assistant and choose Options to open the Office Assistant dialog box.

    c   Clear "Use the Office Assistant" and click OK.

10 Enable shared borders as follows:

    a   Choose Tools, Page Options to open the Page Options dialog box.

    b   Activate the Authoring tab.

    c   Check Shared Borders and click OK.

11 If necessary, reset any FrontPage defaults that you have changed. If you do not wish to reset the defaults, you can still re-key the course, but some activities might not work exactly as documented.

12 Close FrontPage.

13 Choose Start, Programs, Microsoft Office, Microsoft Office Tools. Verify that Microsoft Office Picture Manager appears in the menu.

14 Create a folder named Student Data at the root of the hard drive.

15 If necessary, download the Student Data files for the course. (If you don't have an Internet connection, you can ask your instructor for a copy of the data files on a disk.)

    a Connect to www.courseilt.com/instructor_tools.html.

    b Click the link for Microsoft FrontPage 2003 to display a page of course listings and then click the link for FrontPage 2003: Basic, Second Edition.

    c Click the link for downloading the Student Data files and follow the instructions that appear on your screen.

16 Copy the data files to the Student Data folder.

Unit 1

Getting started

Unit time: 50 minutes

Complete this unit, and you'll know how to:

A Identify important features of the FrontPage environment.

B Identify the tabs in Page view.

Topic A: The FrontPage environment

Explanation   FrontPage 2003 enables you to design, create, and manage dynamic and interactive Web sites. Web pages are based on HTML (Hypertext Markup Language), which is the standard markup language on the Web. With FrontPage, you don't have to type any HTML code manually. When you create and design a Web page, FrontPage automatically generates the HTML code for you.

The FrontPage interface

A *Web site* is a collection of hypertext documents (HTML files), graphics, and media files. FrontPage offers several ways of looking at the information on your Web site. You can use the FrontPage Editor to view the HTML code and preview a page as it would appear in a browser, both in a single view. Exhibit 1-1 shows the elements of the FrontPage window.

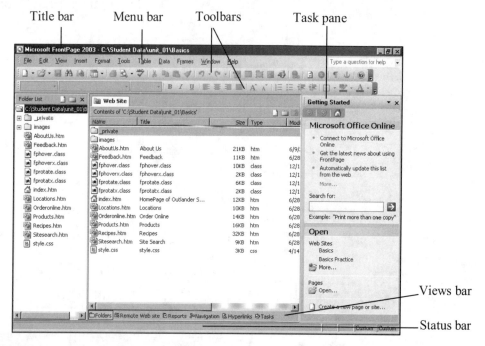

Exhibit 1-1: The FrontPage interface

The following table describes the elements of the FrontPage window:

Element	Description
Title bar	Shows the name of the software followed by the name of the Web site and its location.
Menu bar	Contains menus that you use to work in FrontPage. Each menu has a set of related commands. For example, the Edit menu has options you can use to edit a Web page.
Toolbars	Provide buttons for fast and easy access to various commands.
Views bar	Provides six ways to view your Web site as you work. For example, you can use the Views bar to switch between Hyperlinks, Folders, or Navigation views.
Task pane	Provides options to perform common tasks. For example, you can use the task pane to search for a file, create a new page, or open a Web site.
Status bar	Displays information and messages. For example, Caps Lock and Num Lock indicators appear on the status bar.

Opening a Web site

You need to open a Web site to modify its design or edit its content. When you open a Web site in FrontPage, all the files; HTML pages, images, media files, and any other resources within that Website, are visible and available to you. You can then easily open any individual file within the Web site to edit it. To open a Web site, choose File, Open Site. In the Open Site dialog box, navigate to the folder that contains the Web site, select the Web site, and click Open.

A-1: Examining the FrontPage window

Here's how	Here's why
1 Choose **Start**, **Programs**, **Microsoft Office**, **Microsoft Office FrontPage 2003**	To start Microsoft Office FrontPage.
2 Choose **File**, **Open Site...**	To display the Open Site dialog box so that you can open an existing Web site. A site is a collection of files, graphics, and folders.
Navigate to the current unit folder	(Follow your instructor's directions to find the folder.)
3 Select **Basics**	
Click **Open**	To open the Web site in the FrontPage window.
4 Observe the title bar	The title bar shows the name of the program and the name and location of the site.
5 Observe the menu bar	The menu bar provides options you can use to work with FrontPage.
6 Observe the toolbars	They contain buttons you can use to perform tasks, such as adding a new page, inserting a table, and checking spelling for the entire Web site.
7 Observe the Views bar	On the Views bar, Folders is selected, which means that the current view is the Folders view. This is the default viewing option.
Observe the left pane	It shows the hierarchical list of folders in the current Web site. The first folder, called the root folder, displays the name and location of the Web site. The folder contains the subfolders, *_private* and *images*.
Observe the right pane	It shows a detailed list of the files and folders inside the current Web site.
8 Choose **View**, **Task Pane**	To display the task pane, as shown in Exhibit 1-1. You can use the task pane to perform common actions, such as opening an existing page or creating a new page.
Click ☒	(The Close button is in the upper-right corner of the task pane.) To hide the task pane. You can display it when you want to work with it.

Viewing a Web site in a browser

Explanation

As you're creating a Web site, you can see what it looks like by viewing it either in a browser or right within FrontPage. FrontPage provides a list of available browsers to choose from based on the browsers installed on your computer.

To view a Web site by using Internet Explorer, choose File, Preview in Browser, Microsoft Internet Explorer 5.1 (or later, depending on your computer). You can also choose the resolution of the display screen. As you develop Web sites, it's important to view your results in as many different browsers as possible and at different resolutions. Doing this helps ensure that your design looks the way you intend for your varied Internet audience.

Exhibit 1-2: The Outlander Spices home page

Do it!

A-2:   Viewing a Web site in Internet Explorer

Here's how	Here's why
1 Select **index.htm** in the right pane	
2 Choose **File, Preview in Browser, Microsoft Internet Explorer**	(Maximize the Internet Explorer window, if necessary.) The Web site now appears in Internet Explorer, as shown in Exhibit 1-2. The page contains a brief description of Outlander Spices and links to other pages.
3 Point to **About Us**	
	The shape of the pointer changes to a hand, indicating that the text is a hyperlink.
Click **About Us**	The About Us page appears in the browser.
Scroll down	The page contains a brief introduction to Outlander Spices, its expansion project, and its team members.
4 Scroll up	
Click **Home**	(The Home hyperlink is in the upper-left corner of the page.) To open the home page of the Web site (index.htm).
5 Click **Products**	(The Products hyperlink is on the left side of the page.) To open the Products page. This page contains a list of spices and their prices.
6 Close Internet Explorer	Click the Close button on the upper-right corner of the window.

Hyperlinks view

Explanation

You can use *Hyperlinks view* to see all the hyperlinks of the Web site at a single glance. To switch to Hyperlinks view, click Hyperlinks on the Views bar. In this view, you can click a single page and view all the hyperlinks associated with that page. When you add new hyperlinks to the pages in your Web site, FrontPage automatically updates this view.

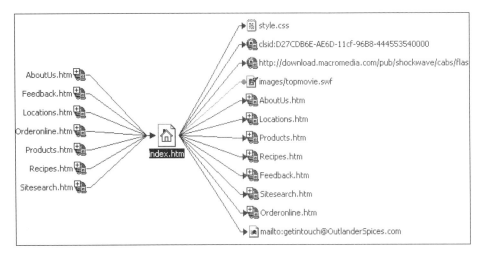

Exhibit 1-3: Hyperlinks view of the Outlander Spices Web site

Do it!

A-3:   Viewing a Web site in Hyperlinks view

Here's how	Here's why
1 On the Views bar, click **Hyperlinks**	To view the Web site in Hyperlinks view, which is divided into two panes.
2 Observe the screen	The right pane displays a diagram of hyperlinks associated with the index.htm page, as shown in Exhibit 1-3. This page contains hyperlinks to all the pages.
3 To the right of Index.htm, observe AboutUs.htm	A plus sign appears on the page icon, indicating that the page has links to other resources.
Click the plus sign	The plus sign changes to a minus sign, and the pages linked to the AboutUs page appear. It shows that the AboutUs page contains hyperlinks to other pages in the Web site.

Navigation view

Explanation

You can create and view the navigation structure of your Web site in *Navigation view*. A *navigation structure* defines the hierarchy of the pages. A good navigation structure provides visitors with a simple and consistent way to move around a site. Exhibit 1-4 shows the navigation structure of the Outlander Spices Web site.

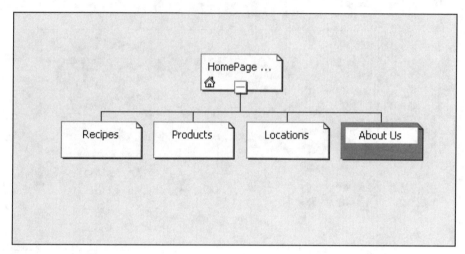

Exhibit 1-4: Navigation view of the Outlander Spices Web site

Do it!

A-4: Viewing a Web site in Navigation view

Here's how	Here's why
1 On the Views bar, click **Navigation**	(To switch to Navigation view.) The window is divided into two panes. The right pane displays a diagram with the home page at the top and the other pages below, as shown in Exhibit 1-4.
Observe the navigation structure of the Web site	The visitor views the home page first. From the home page, the visitor can move to any of the four pages under it.
2 Observe the Navigation toolbar	
	(In the right pane, above the navigation structure.)
Click	(The New Page button is on the Navigation toolbar.) To add a new page to the navigation structure. A new page is added below the About Us page.
3 Click the minus sign on the home page	
	To collapse the pages under HomePage.
Observe the navigation structure	
	The pages under HomePage are collapsed, and a plus sign appears on the home page.

Folders view

Explanation

You access and organize the files and folders of a Web site by using *Folders view*. By default, the following folders are displayed:

- The main folder with the name of the Web site. This is the root folder, and it contains two subfolders named *_private* and *images*.
- The *_private* folder stores form results and other files that are hidden from users.
- The *images* folder stores the images that you use.

In addition to these default folders, you can add as many additional folders as you need. To add a new folder, click the New Folder button and give an appropriate name to the folder. You can also rename an existing folder. To rename a folder, right-click the folder and choose Rename.

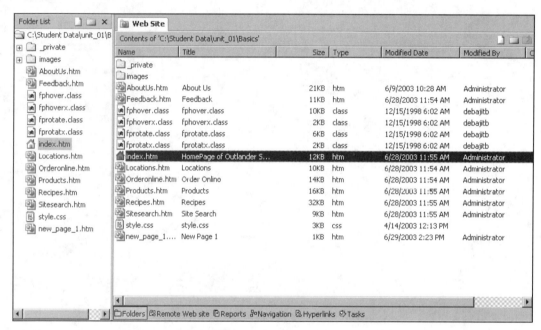

Exhibit 1-5: The Folders view of the Outlander Spices Web site

Shortcut menus

You can right-click on any item to display a shortcut menu. Shortcut menus contain a list of common actions that you can take on the selected item. Using these helps to speed up common or repetitive tasks.

Do it!

A-5: Working in Folders view

Here's how	Here's why
1 Switch to Folders view	(On the Views bar, click Folders.) The window is divided into two panes, as shown in Exhibit 1-5. You use this view to add new folders and rename existing folders.
2 Click 🗀	(The New Folder button is on the upper-right corner of the right pane.) To create a new folder.
Observe the new folder	📄 products.htm 📄 recipes.htm 📄 sitesearch.htm 📄 style.css 🗀 New_Folder A new folder appears in both the panes. Its name is highlighted in the right pane so that you can easily change it.
Click anywhere in the pane	The new folder takes the default name, New_Folder.
3 Right-click **New_Folder**	(In the right pane.) A shortcut menu appears.
Choose **Rename**	
Edit the name of the folder to read **Spices**	
Press ⏎ ENTER	A Rename message box appears briefly.
4 Verify that the Spices folder is selected	
Press DELETE	A message box prompts you to confirm the deletion.
Click **Yes**	To delete the folder.

Topic B: Page view

Explanation

You can make changes or add elements to your Web pages through Page view. You can use the tabs at the bottom of the page to view a page in different ways.

There are four tabs available in Page view:

- Design
- Preview
- Code
- Split

Design view

You can create, edit, or format a page in Design view. To open a page in Design view, double-click the page in the right pane of Folders view. You can also switch to Design view from another view by clicking the Design tab. Design view provides an editing environment that's simple and familiar. Editing in Design view is similar to editing a document in a word processor.

The Toggle Pane button

The Toggle Pane button alternately shows and hides the Folder List in Page view. Deactivating the Folder List creates more space in which to work, and you can easily check the Folder List by clicking the toggle button again.

Do it!

B-1: Exploring a page in Design view

Here's how	Here's why
1 Double-click **AboutUs.htm**	(In the right pane.) To open the document in Page view.
2 Click 🗔	(The Toggle Pane button is on the Standard toolbar.) To hide the Folder List in Page view.
3 Observe the Views bar	[🗔 Design 🗖 Split ⊡ Code 🔍 Preview]
	(The Views bar has buttons you can use to switch quickly from one Web site view to another.) Design view is active by default.

Previewing Web pages

Explanation

With the Preview tab, you can preview a page as it will appear in a browser. You can also use this view to test a component that you've added to a page. However, some components appear only when the Web site is published. You can't make any changes to the page in this view.

Do it!

B-2:   Previewing a page

Here's how	Here's why
1 Click the **Preview** button	
	(At the bottom of the page.) To see the AboutUs page as it would appear in a browser.
2 Click the **All spiced up** link	
	This link leads to another section on the same page. In Preview, pages work the same as they do in a browser.
3 Click anywhere on the page	No insertion point appears, because you can't edit the page in the Preview tab.

Code view

Explanation

When you create a Web page in FrontPage, the program automatically generates the required HTML code. HTML *tags* define the structure of a page. Each tag consists of the tag name surrounded by angular brackets, as shown:

```
<HTML>
```

All Web pages have HTML, HEAD and BODY tags. These are the basic structural tags upon which Web pages are built. These tags consist of a starting tag and an ending tag. For example, <HEAD> is the *starting tag* and </HEAD> is the corresponding *ending tag*. The ending tag is identical to the starting tag, except that it contains a forward slash (/) before the tag name:

```
<HEAD>   </HEAD>
```

The tags that have a starting and a corresponding ending tag are called *containers*. Tags that don't have closing tags are called *empty tags*.

To examine the HTML code in Page view, click the Code tab. If you edit the code in Code view, you can view how the changes look by switching back to Design view. You don't need to know much about HTML coding to use FrontPage effectively, but it certainly helps to have experience with hand coding.

Do it!   **B-3:   Viewing HTML in Code view**

Here's how	Here's why
1 Click the **Code** button	⊡ Code
	(At the bottom of the page.) To activate Code view.
| 2  Observe the Contents pane | ```
1   <html>
2
3   <head>
4   <meta http-equiv="Content-Languag
5   <meta http-equiv="Content-Type" c
6   <meta name="GENERATOR" content="M
7   <meta name="ProgId" content="Fron
8   <title>About Us</title>
9   <link rel="stylesheet" type="text
10
11
12
13  </head>
14
15  <body topmargin="0px" leftmargin=
``` |
	This is the HTML code for the current page. Note that each line of code is numbered for quick reference and ease of use.
3 Observe the first line of code	`<html>`
	This tag marks the beginning of the code for any Web page.
4 Observe the last line of code	`</html>`
	(Scroll to the bottom.) This tag marks the end of the code for the Web page. The entire HTML code is contained between these two tags.
5 Observe the \<head\> tags	(Scroll to the top.) These tags identify the head section of the page. The head section contains the information such as the title and characteristics of the page.
6 Observe the \<title\> tags	`<title>About Us</title>`
	The text within these tags appears on the title bar of the browser window.
7 Observe the \<body\> tags	These tags contain the page content; text, tags, images, and FrontPage components, such as forms and scripts.
```

Split view

Explanation

You can use Split view to view a page in Design view and Code view at the same time. You can make any changes you need in this view. When you make changes in Design view, you can see the corresponding changes in Code view take place at the same time, and vice versa.

You can also use this view to learn HTML because you can see the corresponding code whenever you add or modify elements to a page through Design view.

Exhibit 1-6: The Outlander Spices Web site in Split view

Closing files and Web sites

In FrontPage, the File, Close command closes the active page. To close an entire Web site, choose File, Close Site. To exit the program, you can click the close button in the upper-right corner of the application window, or you can choose File, Exit.

Do it!

B-4: Viewing a page in Split view

Here's how	Here's why
1 Click the **Split** button	To view the page in Code view and Design view simultaneously, as shown in Exhibit 1-6.
2 In the Design view portion, click the heading **All spiced up**	The insertion point appears. The corresponding line in the Code view portion is selected.
3 Choose **File, Close**	To close the page.
Choose **File, Close Site**	To close the Web site.
4 Choose **File, Exit**	To close FrontPage.

Unit summary: Getting started

Topic A   In this topic, you learned how to start FrontPage and explore the **FrontPage environment**. You learned how to view the hyperlinks between pages in **Hyperlinks view** and to preview the navigation structure in **Navigation view**. You also learned how to create and rename folders in **Folders view**.

Topic B   In this topic, you explored the tabs in **Page view**. You learned that you can create a page by using **Design view**, view the HTML code of a page by using **Code view**, preview a page by using **Preview**, and view Design view and Code view simultaneously by using **Split view**.

Independent practice activity

1 Start FrontPage 2003. (If a web page or site opens automatically in FrontPage, close it.)

2 Open the Basics practice Web site (within the current unit folder).

3 Preview the Web site in your browser. (Hint: Select index.htm first.)

4 Briefly browse the site.

5 Close your browser.

6 Open Products.htm in Design view.

7 View the HTML code of Products.htm.

8 View Products.htm simultaneously in Design view and Code view.

9 Close the page.

10 In Folders view, create a new folder and name it **Hot Spices**.

11 Change the folder name from Hot Spices to **Spices**.

12 Close the Web site.

Review questions

1 Which of the following FrontPage elements provides multiple ways to look at your Web site?

   A Views bar

   B Toolbar

   C Task pane

   D Status bar

2   Which of the following commands is used to close an entire Web site?

   A File, Close

   B File, Exit

   C File, Close Site

   D File, Close All

3 Web site files are organized in folders. What is the name of the first, or top-level, folder?

4 What are the four tabs available in Page view?

5 What are some advantages of using Split view?

6 Why is it important to view your Web site in different browsers during the development stage?

Unit 2

Web page fundamentals

Unit time: 80 minutes

Complete this unit, and you'll know how to:

A Create a Web page, add text to a page, and import an existing page into a Web site.

B Set heading and paragraph styles, change text alignment, and add a horizontal line.

C Create a variety of lists, including numbered, bulleted, collapsible, and nested.

D Check spelling throughout a Web site and use the Find and Replace feature.

Topic A: Creating Web pages

Explanation

In this topic, you'll learn how to create a one-page Web site to help you become more familiar with the FrontPage environment and essential features.

The home page

A *home page* is the first page you see when you view a Web site in a browser. It usually provides a welcome message or a statement that describes the purpose of the Web site. In FrontPage, there are several ways in which you can begin building a Web site. One option is to start with a "one-page Web site," which can serve as your home page. From this starting point, you can easily add other pages to your site.

To create a one-page Web site:

1 Choose File, New to display the New task pane.

2 Under New Web site, click One page Web site to open the Web Site Templates dialog box. By default, the General tab is active.

(Alternatively, you can click the arrow next to the New button to display a list. From the list, select Web Site to open the Web Site Templates dialog box.)

3 In the Web Site Templates dialog box, verify that One Page Web Site is selected.

4 Under Options, in the Specify the location of the new Web site box, enter the path and name of your Web site and click OK.

You can also create an empty Web site by selecting Empty Web Site from the Web Site Templates dialog box. Then you can add pages to the Web sites as needed.

Do it!   **A-1:   Creating a one-page Web site**

Here's how	Here's why
1 Choose **File**, **New...**	To display the New task pane.
In the task pane, click **One page Web site**	
	To open the Web Site Templates dialog box.
2 Under the General tab, verify that One Page Web Site is selected	
Under Options, edit the Specify the location of the new Web site box to read **C:\Student Data\ <Current unit folder>\ The spice store**	To specify the title for the Web site. A "The spice store" folder is created in C:\Student Data*<Current unit folder>*.
3 Click **OK**	To create a Web site with a single blank page. The Create New Web message box briefly appears.
4 Observe the folders in the Web site	(Click the Toggle Pane button on the Standard toolbar and choose Folder list, if necessary.) The Web site is created with index.htm as the home page. In addition, the Web site contains two folders, *_private* and *images*.

Within the "Here's how" column, step 1 shows a screenshot:

New Web site
- One page Web site...
- SharePoint team site...
- Web package solutions...
- More Web site templates...

Web page text

Explanation

To add text to a Web page, open the page in Page view, place the insertion point where you want to add the text, and start typing. If the text you need is in another application, such as Microsoft Word or Notepad, you can copy the text from that application and paste it into FrontPage.

For all the text that you enter on a page, FrontPage creates the appropriate HTML tags in the background. As you make changes, you should frequently click the Save button to update your page.

Welcome to Outlander Spices

We bring you a rich heritage of exotic spices from all over the world.

Exhibit 2-1: The home page text after completing step 5

Do it!   **A-2:   Adding text to a Web page**

Here's how	Here's why
1 Double-click **index.htm**	
Switch to split view	(Click the Split button, if necessary.) In the code view pane, you can view the HTML code for the page. There are three basic sets of tags: HTML, HEAD, and BODY.
Click in the Design view pane	To prepare to type text in the page.
2 Type **Welcome to Outlander Spices**	
3 Observe the Code view pane	To view the HTML code. Note that the P tags are added to the code. These tags indicate the beginning and end of a paragraph.
4 Verify that the insertion point is at the end of the sentence	
Press (↵ ENTER)	To move the insertion point to the next paragraph.
5 Type the remaining text	As shown in Exhibit 2-1.
6 Observe the HTML code	All the text that you typed on the page appears between the BODY tags. All visible content on a Web page is entered inside the body section.
Switch to Design view	
7 Click 🖫	(The Save button is on the Standard toolbar.) To save your changes to the page.
Choose **File**, **Close**	

Adding pages to a Web site

Explanation

When you create a new Web site in FrontPage, it generates a home page automatically. Creating additional pages is easy. In the New task pane, click More page templates to open the Page Templates dialog box. (You can also display the Page Templates dialog box by clicking the arrow next to the New button.) Select the type of page you want to create and click OK.

The Save As command

You need to save a Web page to save any changes you make to it. To save a new page, choose File, Save As. In the File name box, specify the name of the page and click Save.

Do it!

A-3:   Adding a new page to a Web site

Here's how	Here's why
1 On the standard toolbar, click the arrow next to the page button	(A list opens.)
From the list, select **Page**	To open the Page Templates dialog box. By default, the General tab is active, and Normal Page is selected. This tab displays a list of all the types of pages that you can create in FrontPage. A normal page is a blank page.
Click **OK**	To open a blank new page.
2 Type the following text: You can now purchase our products from the kiosks located in the states below.	
3 Choose **File**, **Save As...**	To open the Save As dialog box. The current Web folder is active in the Save in list.
Edit the File name box to read **Locations**	To give the page a name.
4 Observe the current page title	(The page title is located above the File name box.) The default text for the title is culled from the first sentence in the page.
Click **Change title**	To display the Set Page Title dialog box.
Edit the Page title box to read **Locations**	
Click **OK**	To close the Set Page Title dialog box and apply the change. The new title will appear on a browser's title bar. It will also appear on the FrontPage title bar after you click Save.
5 Click **Save**	
6 Choose **File**, **Close**	

Importing pages

Explanation

FrontPage makes it easy to import existing pages into a Web site. To import a file:

1 Choose File, Import to open the Import dialog box.
2 Click Add File to open the Add File to Import List dialog box. Navigate to the required folder and select the page that you want to import into the Web site.
3 Click Open to add the page to the Import dialog box, and click OK.

Do it!

A-4: Importing a page into a Web site

Here's how	Here's why
1 Choose **File**, **Import...**	To open the Import dialog box.
2 Click **Add File**	To open the Add File to Import List dialog box.
From the Look in list, select the current unit folder within Student Data	(Follow your instructor's directions.)
Select **Recipe.htm**	(From the current unit folder.)
Click **Open**	To add Recipe.htm to the Import dialog box.
3 Click Add File, select Products.htm, and click Open	To import Products.htm to the Web site.
4 Click **OK**	To import the files into the Web site.
5 Observe the Folder List	Recipe.htm and Products.htm are now a part of the Web site.

Topic B: Page structure and formatting

Explanation

You can enhance the design and readability of a page that contains a lot of text by formatting the content. For example, you can add headings and change the style, color, and size of text. You can also add background colors and images to the page.

Headings and paragraphs

Headings and paragraphs are standard structural components of all kinds of documents, including newspapers, books, and business reports. A heading in a Web page indicates the contents of the page or a section of the page. You can use paragraphs to break large chunks of text into smaller, more readable chunks.

To format a heading or paragraph in a specific style, select the text and then choose the style you want from the Style list on the Formatting toolbar.

About Us
Outlander Spices opened its doors in 1989 and has since become one of the largest spice companies in the world. We provide select gourmet foods and the highest quality spices from all over the world to restaurants and retailers throughout the United States and Europe.
About our spices

Exhibit 2-2: Unformatted text

Heading levels

HTML includes six levels of headings designed to provide structural options for your text content. An H1, or *level-one heading*, is the highest-level heading. It's meant to define the top heading structure for a page. Think of it as the top story headline in a newspaper. An H2, or *level-two heading*, is the next highest, and so on down to H6. Each heading level implies a hierarchical structure.

Browsers apply default font sizes for each of these heading levels. An H1 has the largest font size, and an H6 has the smallest font size. Text in any heading tag is automatically bolded for emphasis.

Exhibit 2-3: The same text, formatted as headings and a paragraph

B-1:   Applying heading and paragraph styles

Here's how	Here's why
1 Open a new blank page	To prepare to create a new page and add text to it.
Save the page as AboutUs.htm	(In the spice store folder, which is in the current unit folder.)
Type in the text shown in Exhibit 2-2	
2 Switch to Split view	
3 Place the insertion point after "About Us"	In the Design pane.

About Us|

Press (↵ ENTER)	
Select the text **About Us**	(Drag over the text.) You'll set this text as the top-level heading.
4 From the Style list, select **Heading 1**	

Normal ▾	Times New
¶ Address	
¶ Bulleted List	
a Default Character Style	
¶ Defined Term	
¶ Definition	
¶ Directory List	
¶ Formatted	
Heading 1	
¶ Heading 2	
¶ Heading 3	
¶ Heading 4	
¶ Heading 5	
¶ Heading 6	
¶ Menu List	
¶ Normal	
¶ Numbered List	

	The Style list is the first list on the Formatting toolbar. The size of the text increases to the default text size for an H1 tag.
Observe the HTML code	H1 tags are added to the About Us text.

5 Display the Font Color palette

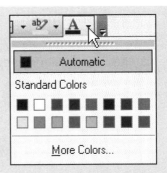

(Click the arrow as shown here.)

    Select a color

    Deselect the text   The text appears with your chosen color.

    Observe the HTML code   FONT tags are added to the code, with a COLOR attribute that specifies the hexadecimal number for the color.

6 Place the insertion point before the text "About our spices"

> |About our spices

    Press (↵ ENTER)

    Select the text **About our spices**

    From the Style list, select **Heading 2**

    Deselect the text   The text now appears as Heading 2, as shown in Exhibit 2-3.

7 Observe the HTML code   The H2 tags are added to the About our spices text.

    Save your changes

Text alignment

Explanation

By default, text is always aligned to the left side of a page. You can use the alignment buttons on the Formatting toolbar to change the alignment of any text element. Your options are left, center, right, and justify.

Exhibit 2-4: Alignment options: Left (default), center, right, and justify

Do it!

B-2: Aligning text

Here's how	Here's why
1 Select the "About Us" text	**About Us**
2 Click ☰	To center-align the text.
Observe the HTML code	The ALIGN attribute is added to the H1 tag, showing the value "center."
3 Select the paragraph under "About Us"	
4 Click ☰	To justify the paragraph.
5 Save your changes	

Horizontal lines

Explanation

As shown in Exhibit 2-5, you can divide the contents of a page visually into different sections by inserting a horizontal line (also known as a *horizontal rule*). To insert a horizontal line in a page, place the insertion point where you want the line to appear and then choose Insert, Horizontal Line.

You can then change the width, height, alignment, or color of the line by changing its properties. You can display the Properties dialog box for a horizontal line or any other object by selecting it and then choosing Format, Properties. You can also display the properties by right-clicking the line and choosing the Properties command from the shortcut menu that appears.

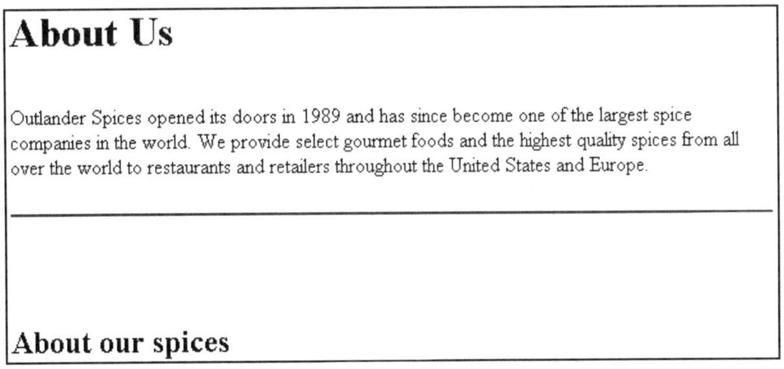

About Us

Outlander Spices opened its doors in 1989 and has since become one of the largest spice companies in the world. We provide select gourmet foods and the highest quality spices from all over the world to restaurants and retailers throughout the United States and Europe.

About our spices

Exhibit 2-5: A page showing a horizontal line

B-3: Inserting a horizontal line

Here's how	Here's why
1 Place the insertion point as shown	ghest quality spices fro tes and Europe.
2 Choose **Insert**, **Horizontal Line**	A horizontal line appears below the text.
3 Observe the HTML code	The HR tag creates a horizontal line. It's an empty tag, so it has no closing tag.
4 Select the line	
Choose **Format, Properties**	

Horizontal Line Properties

Size
Width: 100 ◉ Percent of window ○ Pixels
Height: 2 Pixels

Alignment
○ Left ◉ Center ○ Right

Color:
■ Automatic ▼ ☐ Solid line (no shading)

Style...   OK   Cancel

To open the Horizontal Line Properties dialog box.

5 From the Color list, select a color	
Click **OK**	To apply the color to the line.
Deselect the line	The line takes on your chosen color.
6 Observe the HTML code	The COLOR attribute is added to the HR tag.
7 Save and close the page	

Formatting text

Explanation

To apply formatting to text, select the text and use the Formatting toolbar to change its font, size, style, or color. You can also use the Format, Font command to display the Font dialog box. This dialog box contains formatting options that aren't available on the toolbar.

Although you can select specific fonts, the way the Web page appears depends on the browser and available fonts of each individual visitor to your Web site. For this reason, it's a good idea to test your Web pages in several different browsers.

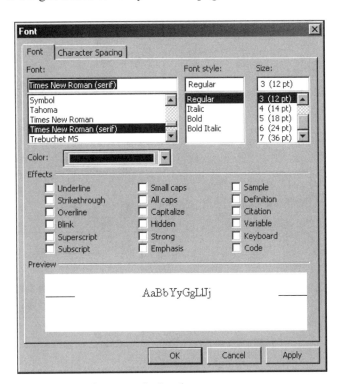

Exhibit 2-6: The Font dialog box

Do it!

B-4:   Changing text styles

Here's how	Here's why
1 Open index.htm	
2 Select the text on the first line	
3 From the Font list, select **Arial Black**	(On the Formatting toolbar.)
Observe the HTML code	The text now appears between the FONT tags, and the FACE attribute specifies the name of the font.
4 From the Font Size list, select **4 (14 pt)**	(On the Formatting toolbar.) To increase the size of the text.
Observe the HTML code	(The SIZE attribute is added to the FONT tag. The value assigned is 4 indicating that the size of the text corresponds to 14 points.)
5 Display the Font Color palette	
	(The Font Color button is on the Formatting toolbar.)
Select a color	
Deselect the text	The text takes on your chosen color.

6 Observe the HTML code	The COLOR attribute is added to the FONT tag. The value assigned to it specifies the color of the text.
7 Select the text on the second line	
8 Choose **Format**, **Font...**	The Font dialog box appears, as shown in Exhibit 2-6.
Observe the options in the Font dialog box	You can change the font style, size, color, and effects in this dialog box.
Under Font style, select **Italic**	
Click **OK**	
Observe the HTML code	The I tag is added within the P tag.
9 Save your changes and close the page	

Rulers

Explanation

You can use a ruler to help you to arrange your page content. For example, to align the text under a heading to a specific point, a ruler can help you be more precise. To view your page with a ruler, choose View, Ruler and Grid, Show Ruler.

Do it!

B-5: Applying rulers

Here's how	Here's why
1 Open Recipe.htm	
Switch to Design view	
2 Choose **View**, **Ruler and Grid**, **Show Ruler**	The ruler appears on the page.
Place the insertion point directly before the 3, as shown	
	The ruler shows the position of the text at about 240.
3 Press (SPACEBAR) three times	To align the quantity of ingredients to a more precise visual reference point, 250.
Observe the reading on the ruler	The ruler shows the position of the text as 250.

4 Change the alignment of all the other ingredient amounts, using 250 as your reference point

Almonds, blanched peeled and sliced	3 tbsp
Outlander Spices Cinnamon powder	1 ½ tsp
Outlander Spices Nutmeg powder	1 ½ tsp
Outlander Spices Coriander powder	1 ½ tsp
Outlander Spices Red chili powder	3 tsp
Oil	1/2cup
Onions chopped	1/2cup
Ginger paste	2 tsp
Garlic paste	2 tsp

5 Choose **View**, **Ruler and Grid**, **Show Ruler**   To hide the ruler.

6 Save your changes

Topic C: Working with lists

Explanation

Lists provide an effective way to arrange information. Some types of content are more suited to a list format than to a paragraph or a series of paragraphs. Depending on the purpose, you can create various types of lists, including bulleted lists, numbered lists, multilevel lists, definition lists, and collapsible lists.

Bulleted lists

Bulleted lists (also known as *unordered lists*) are intended to display items of more or less equal importance. For example, you can use a bulleted list to describe the advantages of a particular product. Generally, simple shapes such as squares or circles represent bullets in these lists.

To create a bulleted list, select the text you want to convert into a bulleted list and click the Bullets button. If you want to control the appearance of the bullets, you can choose the Bullets and Numbering option from the Format menu.

Do it!

C-1: Creating a bulleted list

Here's how	Here's why
1 Select the ingredients	Almonds, blanched peeled and sliced 3 tbsp **Outlander Spices** Cinnamon powder 1 ½ tsp **Outlander Spices** Nutmeg powder 1 ½ tsp **Outlander Spices** Coriander powder 1 ½ tsp **Outlander Spices** Red chili powder 3 tsp Oil 1/2cup Onions chopped 1/2cup Ginger paste 2 tsp Garlic paste 2 tsp
2 Click 📋	(The Bullets button is on the Formatting toolbar.) The text now appears as a bulleted list.
3 Locate the list tags in the HTML code	(Switch to Code view.) UL tags are added to the code. The UL tags indicate that the list is an unordered list. The LI tags define each item in the list.
Switch to Design view	
Click anywhere on the page	To deselect the text.
4 Save your changes	

Numbered lists

Explanation

Numbered lists (also known as *ordered lists*) display items in sequence or items of descending importance. For example, you can represent steps to accomplish a specific task as a numbered list. Each item in the list is marked with a number or a letter.

To create a numbered list, select the text you want to convert into a list and click the Numbering button. If you want to use a different numbering style, you can use the Format, Bullets and Numbering command.

Do it!

C-2:   Creating a numbered (ordered) list

Here's how	Here's why
1 Select the recipe instructions	Whisk the yoghurt with the roasted paste. Mix well. Heat the oil: reduce the heat, add onions, ginger and garlic pastes. Fry until golden brown. Add the potatoes and fry until golden brown. Add the yoghurt and mix the salt. Cook for 5 minutes and then add ¾ cup of warm water. Bring to a boil, reduce heat, and cook until the potatoes are tender and the gravy is thick.
Click	(The Numbering button is on the Formatting toolbar.) The text now appears as a numbered list.
2 Locate the list tags in the HTML code	(Scroll down, if necessary.) OL tags are added to the code. OL tags indicate that the list is an ordered list.
Switch to Design view	
3 Save and close the page	

Nested lists

Explanation

You can use a nested list to display data of various levels, as you might see in an outline. You can create lists that have multiple nested levels and paragraphs. Each level can have a bulleting style that is different from the others. You create a multilevel list by creating a bulleted or numbered list and then indenting the sublevels. You can indent the sublevels by using the Increase Indent button on the Formatting toolbar. You can also collapse the lists to show only the top-level item. Then, when you click the top-level item, the other items appear.

Exhibit 2-7: A nested list

Do it!

C-3: Creating a nested list

Here's how	Here's why
1 Open Products.htm	
2 Select the text **Spices - Whole**	
Click [icon]	
3 Select the spices	
Click [icon]	To make the spices into list items.
Click [icon] twice	To create a multilevel list.
Deselect the text	
	The nested list visually indicates that the spices are a subset of "Spices – Whole."

4 Locate the list tags in the HTML code	There are UL tags nested inside the outer UL tags.
5 Switch to Design view	
Select the text **Spices – Whole**	
6 Choose **Format**, **Bullets and Numbering...**	To open the List Properties dialog box. The Plain Bullets tab is active and the current bullet style is selected by default.
Check **Enable Collapsible Outlines**	
Check **Initially Collapsed**	
7 Click **OK**	
8 Click the **Preview** button	(The collapsible list effect can be viewed in the Preview but not in Design view.)
Observe the bulleted list	**Products** • Spices - Whole Spices - Powdered
	The items below Spices – Whole are not visible by default.
Click **Spices – Whole**	The list items appear.
Click the same text again	The items are now hidden.
Switch to Design view	
9 Save your changes	

Definition lists

Explanation

If you need to define terms or to create a list, such as series of items and their descriptions, you can use a definition list to provide your structure, as shown in Exhibit 2-8. To create a definition list:

1   Place the insertion point where you want the list to begin.

2   From the Style list, select Defined Term, and then type the term to be defined.

3   Press Enter to complete the defined term, and then type the definition. The style automatically changes from Defined Term to Definition.

4   Press Enter again to type the next term.

5   Continue this for all the terms that you want to define.

6   Press Enter twice to end the list.

Spices - Powdered

Cumin
  Cumin is common to Indian and Middle Eastern cuisine. With its strong flavor and pungency, it is a prominent ingredient in curries.
Star Anise
  Star anise has a powerful, licorice-like flavor. It is native to many eastern countries including China, Vietnam, and Japan.
Pepper
  A popular flavoring for sauces, meats and marinades, pepper is one of the most common spices used in cuisines across the globe.
Coriander
  This is a great spice for all kinds of things. It can be used as salad dressings and a sweet spice to go with apples, cauliflower, cabbage, or in a curry.

Exhibit 2-8: A definition list

Definition lists are made up of DL tags, which contain a series of DT tags, which hold each defined term. The description for each defined term is contained in a DD tag. By default, browsers indent text in a DD tag.

Do it!

C-4: Creating a definition list

Here's how	Here's why
1 Place the insertion point after "Spices – Powdered"	○ Cloves **Spices - Powdered|**
	To prepare to create a definition list for powdered spices.
2 Press (↵ ENTER)	To move the insertion point to the next line.
3 From the Style list, select **Defined Term**	This sets the structure for the defined term.
Type **Cumin**	To prepare to define this term.
Switch to Split view	The DL tags are added to the code, indicating that this is a definition list. The DT tags hold the defined terms.
4 Press (↵ ENTER)	Note that the insertion point is indented and the style in the Style list is Definition.
Type **Cumin is common to Indian and Middle Eastern cuisine. With its strong flavor and pungency, it is a prominent ingredient in curries.**	To provide a description for Cumin.
Observe the HTML code	The DD tags hold each item's definition, or description.
Press (↵ ENTER)	In the Style list, the style changes to Defined Term.
5 Type the rest of the text, as shown in Exhibit 2-8.	
Switch to Design view	
6 Save your changes and close the page	
Close the Web site	

Topic D: Proofing tools

Explanation

Everyone makes occasional spelling mistakes, or typos, as they enter text. FrontPage offers proofing tools to correct these. You can check for spelling errors quickly and easily, just as you can with a word processing application. You can also use the Find and Replace feature to change all instances of a word globally on a page or across all the pages of your Web site.

Spell checking

To check for spelling errors and typos:

1   Switch to Folders view and click ![ABC spelling icon]. The Spelling dialog box appears. From here, you can check either the entire Web site or a selected page.

2   Select the option you want and click Start. The dialog box expands to show a list of pages containing words that aren't in the FrontPage dictionary.

3   For each page, you can correct spelling errors by double-clicking the page to display a second spelling dialog box that shows you each questionable word, one at a time.

4   For each word that isn't in the FrontPage dictionary, you can choose to change the spelling, ignore it, or add the word to the dictionary. When you finish checking all the words on a page, you're given the option to continue with other pages. When all words are accounted for, a message appears informing you that the spell checking is complete.

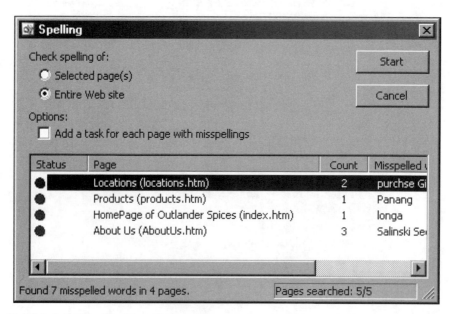

Exhibit 2-9: The Spelling dialog box

Do it!

D-1: Spell checking

Here's how	Here's why
1 Open the Outlander Spices Web site	(From the current unit folder.)
2 Switch to Folders view	(If necessary.)
3 Click ![ABC spell check icon]	To open the Spelling dialog box.
Select **Entire Web site**	To check the spelling of every page in the site.
4 Click **Start**	The dialog box displays a list of all pages that contain spelling errors or words not in the FrontPage dictionary, as shown in Exhibit 2-9.
5 Double-click **Locations (Locations.htm)**	The Locations page appears in the background with the word "purchse" selected. The dialog box suggests "purchase" as a possible correction.
6 Observe the buttons in the Spelling dialog box	You can choose to change the selected word, ignore it, or add it to the dictionary. In this case, you want to change it to the suggested word.
Click **Change**	To change the spelling of "purchse" to "purchase."
7 Observe the Spelling dialog box	The next word found is "Givo", which is somebody's name. In this case, you want to ignore this word wherever it appears.
Click **Ignore All**	Most names don't appear in the dictionary, and it will save you time if you choose to ignore all instances of a name when the spell checker finds it.
8 Click **Next Page**	In the next page, the first word found is also a name.
9 Ignore all instances of all the names	The Continue with the next page? dialog box appears.
Check the spellings of the next pages	The Finished checking pages dialog box appears.
10 Click **Back To List**	To close the Finished checking pages dialog box and return to the Spelling dialog box.
11 Observe the Spelling dialog box	The page status is now marked as Edited.
Click Cancel	To close the Spelling dialog box.

Find and Replace

Explanation

FrontPage's Find and Replace feature allows you to find a specific word in a document or throughout a Web site and replace it with another word. To find and replace a word:

1   Choose Edit, Replace to open the Find and Replace dialog box.

2   In the Find what box, enter the word you want to find.

3   In the Replace box, enter your replacement word.

4   Click Find in Site to begin replacing the word. The pages containing the word you want to replace appear at the bottom of the dialog box.

5   Double-click a page to begin finding instances of the word to be replaced. For each instance of the word, you can choose to replace it, replace all the instances in the page, skip it (by clicking Find Next), or return to the Web site. When you finish, the status for each page is marked as edited.

Do it!   **D-2:   Using Find and Replace**

Here's how	Here's why
1 Choose **Edit**, **Replace...**	To open the Find and Replace dialog box. By default, the Replace tab is active.
2 In the Find what box, enter **VP**	To locate all instances of "VP."
In the Replace with box, enter **Vice President**	To prepare to replace all instances of "VP" with "Vice President."
Under Find where, select **All pages**	(If necessary.) To find the word "VP" in all the pages in the Web site.
3 Click **Find in Site**	A list of the pages displays. The listed pages contain the word and the number of instances it is displayed. In this case, there is only one page containing this text.
4 Double-click **About Us (AboutUs.htm)**	The page appears in Design view.
5 Click **Replace**	To replace the word "VP" with "Vice President."
Click **Replace** again, twice	To replace the next occurrences of the word. (The Finished checking pages dialog box appears.)
6 Click **Back To List**	The status of the page in the dialog box is now marked as Edited.
Close the Find and Replace dialog box	
Close the Web site	

Unit summary: Web page fundamentals

Topic A   In this topic, you learned how to create a **one-page Web site**. You learned how to add text to a page and how to add a new blank page to a Web site. You also learned how to import an existing page to a Web site.

Topic B   In this topic, you learned how to set **paragraph and heading styles** by using the Formatting toolbar. You also learned how to **align and format text** by using the Formatting toolbar and how to add a **horizontal line** to a page. You also learned how to use a **ruler** to help you to more precisely arrange content.

Topic C   In this topic, you learned how to add **bulleted**, **numbered**, **nested**, **collapsible, and definition lists** to a page.

Topic D   Finally, you learned how to **check spelling** throughout a Web site. You also learned how to use **Find and Replace** to search for a specific word and replace it with another word.

Independent practice activity

1   Create a one-page Web site called **Practice Web** in the current unit folder, which is located in Student Data.

2   Add a blank new page and add the text "Your order has been recorded."

3   In the next line, enter the text "Thanks for ordering from Outlander Spices."

4   Set the text "Your order has been recorded" as a level-one heading (H1). Change the heading text color and align it to the center.

5   Add a horizontal line, as shown in Exhibit 2-10, and give it a color of your choice.

6   Format the text, "Thanks for ordering from Outlander Spices," with the font of your choice, and give it a new text color.

7   Set the title of the page to **Thank you**. (Hint: Open the Save As dialog box and click the Change title tab. Then, edit the Page title box.)

8   Save the page as **Thanks.htm**.

9   Close the page.

10   Import the **Orderonline.htm** page to the Web site.

11   Create a new page and create a definition list as shown in Exhibit 2-11. Save the page as **PracticeProducts**.

12   Find **Outleander** and replace it with **Outlander** throughout the Web site.

13   Close the Web site.

> # Your order has been recorded.
>
> ---
>
> **Thanks for ordering from** Outlander Spices.

Exhibit 2-10: Text messages with a horizontal line

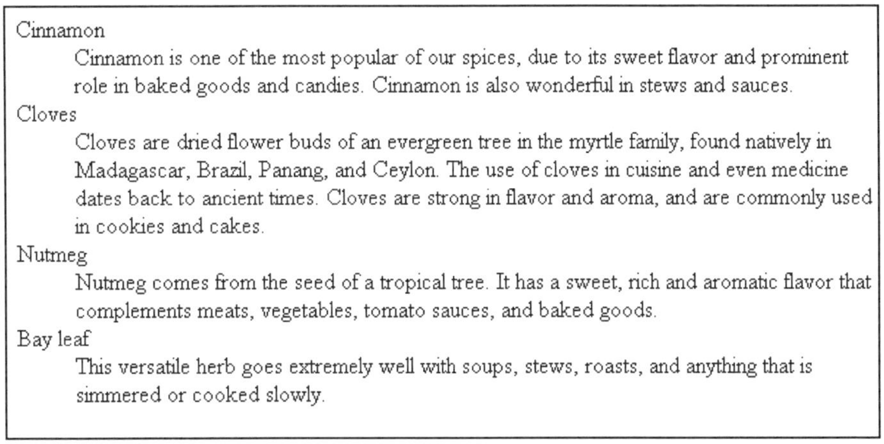

Cinnamon
> Cinnamon is one of the most popular of our spices, due to its sweet flavor and prominent role in baked goods and candies. Cinnamon is also wonderful in stews and sauces.

Cloves
> Cloves are dried flower buds of an evergreen tree in the myrtle family, found natively in Madagascar, Brazil, Panang, and Ceylon. The use of cloves in cuisine and even medicine dates back to ancient times. Cloves are strong in flavor and aroma, and are commonly used in cookies and cakes.

Nutmeg
> Nutmeg comes from the seed of a tropical tree. It has a sweet, rich and aromatic flavor that complements meats, vegetables, tomato sauces, and baked goods.

Bay leaf
> This versatile herb goes extremely well with soups, stews, roasts, and anything that is simmered or cooked slowly.

Exhibit 2-11: The definition list

Review questions

1 Which of the following is used to help you align text on the page?

A Heading

B Horizontal line

C Ruler

D List

2 How many HTML heading levels are available?

3 What is the procedure that is used to import a file into a Web page?

4 How is the appearance of the six heading levels determined?

5 Which of the following type of list is used to specifically display items in sequence?

A Bulleted

B Numbered

C Nested

D Definition

Unit 3

Hyperlinks

Unit time: 70 minutes

Complete this unit and you'll know how to:

A Create a hyperlink, create and link to a bookmark, and test links in Design view.

B Link to an external page on the Internet and create an e-mail link.

C Create a navigation structure, and add and test a navigation bar.

D Test and update hyperlinks.

Topic A: Internal links

Explanation

Hyperlinks are perhaps the most important function of Web pages. They allow us to move from one page to another within a Web site or to jump to another Web site or resource on another server. *Internal links* are hyperlinks that link files within a Web site. FrontPage makes it easy to create and test such hyperlinks.

Linking to another page

You can easily create hyperlinks that connect the pages in your Web site. To create a hyperlink, select the text and choose Insert, Hyperlink to open the Create Hyperlink dialog box. Select the name of the page to which you want to link and click OK.

After you create the hyperlink, you can format the hyperlink text just as you can change any other text. By default, hyperlinks are underlined and blue. You can remove the underlining and blue color by using the standard formatting options.

Do it!   **A-1:   Creating a link to another page**

Here's how	Here's why
1 Open the Hyperlinks Web site	(From the current unit folder.)
2 Open index.htm	
Switch to Split view	If necessary.
3 Select the text **About Us**	(On the left side of the page.)
Observe the HTML code	`<a href="AboutUs.htm">About Us</a>`
	The A tags create a hyperlink. The text enclosed within this link tag appears as the hyperlink. The HREF attribute specifies the page to which the hyperlink will lead. Here, the text About Us links to AboutUs.htm.
Switch to Design view	
4 Select the text **Locations**	You'll create a hyperlink on this text and link it to Locations.htm.
5 Click 🖼	(The Insert Hyperlink button is on the Standard toolbar.) To open the Insert Hyperlink dialog box. The names of all the pages in the Web site appear in the dialog box.
Select **Locations.htm**	
Click **OK**	To create the hyperlink.
6 Switch to Split view	
Observe the HTML code	The text "Locations" is set inside a link tag.
Switch to Design view	
7 Save your changes	

Testing hyperlinks

Explanation

You can test hyperlinks either by previewing the page in a browser or by using the Preview tab. You can test a link in Design view by using the Follow Hyperlink command in the shortcut menu for the link. You can also test links by holding down the Ctrl key and clicking the link.

Do it!

A-2:   Testing hyperlinks in Design view

Here's how	Here's why
1 Right-click **Locations**	To display the shortcut menu as shown.

> Cut
> Copy
> Paste
> Follow Hyperlink
> Insert Rows
> Insert Columns
> Split Cells...
> Open Page in New Window
> Manage Editable Regions...
> Cell Properties...
> Table Properties...
> Page Properties...
> Font...
> Hyperlink Properties...

Choose **Follow Hyperlink**	To open the Locations page.
2 Right-click **Home**	
Choose **Follow Hyperlink**	To return to the home page.
3 Close the index.htm and Locations.htm pages	

Bookmarks

Explanation

You can use a bookmark to create a link to another section of a page. To do this, you create a bookmark on any text on a page and then create a hyperlink that points to that bookmark. Bookmarks work the same way that other hyperlinks do. The difference is that bookmarks are linked to other sections of the same page. This technique is useful for long pages divided into different sections. To create and link to a bookmark:

1   Select the text you want to set as a bookmark.

2   Choose Insert, Bookmark to open the Bookmark dialog box.

3   Name the bookmark and click OK.

4   Select the text you want to link to the bookmark and open the Insert Hyperlink dialog box.

5   Click the Bookmark button to open the Select Place in Document dialog box.

6   From the list of available bookmarks, select the bookmark you want and click OK.

Do it!

A-3:   Creating and linking to a bookmark

Here's how	Here's why
1 Open AboutUs.htm	
2 Scroll down	
Select the text **The Project team**	To make our dreams come ... project team of professional ... successfully. The team is w... the next two years. The Project team (The text is near the bottom of the page.)
3 Choose **Insert, Bookmark...**	To open the Bookmark dialog box. (By default, the bookmark name appears as The_Project_team.)
Click **OK**	To create the bookmark. FrontPage gives the selected text a dashed underline to indicate that it's a bookmark.
4 Observe the HTML code	

`<td height="20px">`
`  <h5><a name="The Project team">The Project team</a></h5>`
`</td>`	

	The text is now enclosed within the A tags. The NAME attribute defines the name of the bookmark.
Switch to Design view	

5 Scroll up

   Select the text
   The Project team

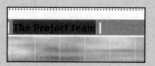

(The text is towards the top of the page.) You want to create a hyperlink from this text to the bookmark.

6 Click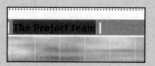

   To open the Insert Hyperlink dialog box.

   Click **Bookmark**

   To open the Select Place in Document dialog box.

   From the list of bookmarks, select
   The_Project_team

   To link to this bookmark.

   Click **OK**

   To return to the Insert Hyperlink dialog box.

   Click **OK**

   To create the hyperlink.

7 Observe the HTML code

   The HREF attribute of the A tag shows the target of the hyperlink. The number sign (#) indicates that the target is within the same page.

   Switch to Design view

8 Hold down Ctrl and click the hyperlink at the top of the page

   To verify that the bookmark link works correctly. The page jumps to the Project Team heading.

9 Save and close the page

Topic B: External links

Explanation   You can create hyperlinks to other Web sites on the Internet, and you can create e-mail links that provide your visitors with an easy way to send you or another contact person an e-mail message.

Linking to an external Web site

To create a hyperlink to an external resource, select the text you want to serve as the hyperlink and choose Insert, Hyperlink to open the Insert Hyperlink dialog box. In the Address box, enter the URL of the Web site and click OK to create the hyperlink.

Do it!   ### B-1:   Linking to another Web site

Here's how	Here's why
1 Open Products.htm	
2 Scroll down	
Select the text "Find more information about these spices"	(The text is just above the copyright statement at the bottom of the page.)
3 Open the Insert Hyperlink dialog box	
In the Address box, enter **http://www.msn.com**	To link to the Microsoft Search Network Web site.
Click **OK**	To create the hyperlink.
4 Observe the HTML code	The HREF attribute of the link tag shows that the text is linked to http://www.msn.com.
Switch to Design view	
5 Save and close the page	

Linking to an e-mail address

Explanation

Many Web sites have links that allow users to send an e-mail quickly and easily with questions or feedback about the Web site. You can create hyperlinks that activate a user's e-mail application and create a new e-mail form set to a specific address. These links are called *e-mail links*, or *mailto links*. To create an e-mail hyperlink:

1 Select the text you want to serve as the hyperlink.

2 Choose Insert, Hyperlink to open the Insert Hyperlink dialog box.

3 Under Link to, select E-mail Address.

4 Enter the e-mail address in the E-mail address box. If you want to add a default subject line to the e-mail, enter it in the Subject box.

5 Click OK to create the hyperlink.

Do it!

B-2: Creating an e-mail link

Here's how	Here's why
1 Open index.htm	
Select the text **Contact Us**	(On the left side of the page.)
2 Open the Insert Hyperlink dialog box	
3 Under Link to, select **E-mail Address**	(In the left pane of the dialog box.)
In the E-mail address box, enter **getintouch@ outlanderspices.com**	E-mail address: mailto:getintouch@outlanderspices.com The hyperlink will send an e-mail to this address. Note that "mailto:" is automatically prefixed to the e-mail address.
Click **OK**	
Switch to Design view	If necessary.
Save and close the page	

Topic C: Navigation bars and shared borders

Explanation

One of the most important facets of effective Web design is a consistent navigation structure. FrontPage makes it easy to create navigation bars that are consistent across all pages in a Web site, so that users can easily find what they're looking for.

Navigation structure

A *navigation structure* defines the hierarchy of the pages in a Web site. For example, the navigation structure of the Outlander Spices Web site is shown in Exhibit 3-1.

A *navigation bar* is a set of links to various parts of a Web site that appears on most or all of the pages in the Web site. FrontPage creates navigation bars based on the site's navigation structure. You can create a navigation structure in Navigation view by dragging files from the left pane to the right. When you drag a file below an existing file, FrontPage adds lines linking the two files in the structure.

If you move files between folders, links and other references might be broken. But FrontPage compensates for this possibility by automatically updating the destination of all hyperlinks.

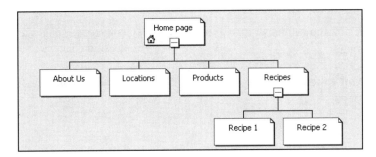

Exhibit 3-1: Sample navigation structure

Do it!

C-1: Creating a navigation structure

Here's how	Here's why
1 Choose **View, Navigation**	To switch to Navigation view.
Display the Folder List	(If necessary.) Choose View, Folder List
2 Drag **AboutUs.htm** from the left pane to the right pane, as shown	
3 Drag Locations.htm, Products.htm, and Recipes.htm to the right pane	(As shown in Exhibit 3-1.) Drag these files from the left pane to the right pane to form the navigation structure.
Drag Recipe1.htm and Recipe2.htm below Recipes	(The final navigation structure should appear as shown in Exhibit 3-1.)
4 Click the minus sign on the home page	To collapse the pages under the home page. The minus sign changes to a plus sign.
Click the plus sign on the home page	To expand the navigation structure.

Shared borders

Explanation

Once you've defined the navigation structure, the next step is to define *shared borders* for your pages. Shared borders are areas in the margins that contain the same elements on all the pages in the Web site. This establishes consistency in your navigation scheme. To define shared borders, choose Format, Shared Borders, and specify where you want shared borders to appear and whether they should appear on all pages or just the current page. To create navigation bars:

1 Place the insertion point within a shared border area.

2 Choose Insert, Navigation to open the Insert Web Component dialog box.

3 Select the type of navigation bar you want.

4 Select the style and orientation of the bar in the subsequent dialog boxes.

5 Click Finish to open the Link Bar Properties dialog box.

6 Specify which levels of the navigation structure to include in the bars and click OK.

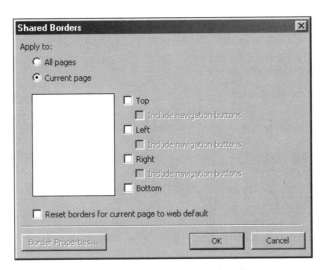

Exhibit 3-2: The Shared Borders dialog box

C-2: Creating a shared border and a navigation bar

Here's how	Here's why
1 Double-click **About Us**	(In the right pane.) To open the page in Design view. You first create a shared border and then insert a navigation bar, so that they appear on all pages.
2 Choose **Format**, **Shared Borders...**	To open the Shared Borders dialog box, as shown in Exhibit 3-2.
Under Apply to, select **All pages**	To include shared borders on all pages in the Web site.
Check **Bottom**	To display the shared border at the bottom of the page.
Click **OK**	The shared border appears at the bottom of the page. You can edit the properties of the shared border to include either comments or a navigation bar in the shared border.
3 Click the comment text	Comment: Shared Bottom Border
	(At the bottom of the page.) The shape of the pointer changes to a pointing finger. The entire line is selected.
Press (DELETE)	To prepare to insert a navigation bar here.
4 Choose **Insert**, **Navigation...**	To open the Insert Web Component dialog box.
Under Component type, verify that Link Bars is selected	
Under Choose a bar type, select **Bar based on navigation structure**	
Click **Next**	To prepare to select a bar style.

5 Verify that a bar style is selected

Use Page's Theme

(This is the default style.)

   Click **Next**   To prepare to select an orientation for the links.

6 Verify that the indicated option is selected

In this orientation, links are arranged horizontally.

   Click **Finish**   The Link Bar Properties dialog box appears. By default, the General tab is activated.

7 Under Hyperlinks to add to page, select **Child pages under Home**

To include all the pages directly under the home page.

   Under Additional pages, check **Home page**

To include a link to the home page in the navigation bar.

   Click **OK**   The page now has a navigation bar with the names of the pages linked to it in the shared border.

8	Right-click on the shared border	To open the shortcut menu.
	Choose **Shared Border Properties...**	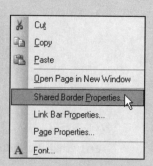
		To open the Border Properties dialog box.
	Under Background, check **Color**	
	Click the arrow next to Color	To prepare to select a suitable background color for the shared border.
	Click **More Colors**	To open the More Colors dialog box.
	Select the indicated color	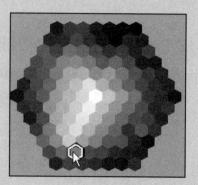
	Click **OK**	To close the More Colors dialog box.
	Click **OK**	To apply the changes and close the Border Properties dialog box.
9	Deselect the shared border	The selected color appears as the background.
10	Save and close the page	

Remove shared borders

Explanation   After inserting shared borders in all pages in the Web site, you might need to remove a shared border from a specific page of your Web site. To remove shared borders, choose Format, Shared Borders to open the Shared Borders dialog box. Under Apply to, select All pages or Current page and then uncheck Top, Left, Right, or Bottom, depending on the position of the shared border, and click OK.

Do it!   ## C-3:   Removing shared borders

Here's how	Here's why
1 Open Recipes.htm	To prepare to remove the shared border from this page.
2 Choose Format, Shared Borders	To open the Shared Borders dialog box.
Under Apply to, select **Current page**	
Uncheck **Bottom**	
Click **OK**	To remove the shared border from this page. The page no longer has the shared borders.
3 Save and close the page	
4 Remove shared borders from the Feedback.htm page	Open Feedback.htm, then open the Shared Border dialog box, select Current page, uncheck Bottom, and click OK.
5 Save and close the page	

Testing navigation bars

Explanation

After you create a navigation bar, test it to verify that it's functioning as you intend it to. You can test a navigation bar in Preview view or in a Web browser. To test a navigation bar in a browser, open the page in a browser and click through the links.

Do it!

C-4: Testing a navigation bar

Here's how	Here's why
1 Open AboutUs.htm in your browser	Select it in the Folder List, then choose File, Preview in Browser, Microsoft Internet Explorer.
2 Click the **Products** link at the bottom of the page	The Products page appears in the browser window.
3 Go back to the home page	Click the hyperlink Home in the navigation bar at the bottom of the page.
4 Minimize the browser window	

Custom links bar

Explanation

As you create a links bar based on your navigation structure, you can also create a links bar with custom links. You do not need to have a predefined structure to create a custom links bar. To create a links bar with custom links:

1 Choose Insert, Navigation to open the Insert Web Component dialog box.

2 In the left pane, select Link Bars, and in the right pane, select Bar with custom links.

3 Click Next to move to the next dialog box, select a bar style and orientation, and click Finish.

4 In the Create New Link Bar dialog box, enter a name for the links bar, and click OK to open the Link Bar Properties dialog box.

5 Click the Add link button to open the Add to Link Bar dialog box and select the pages to which you want to link.

6 Add all the pages to which you want these links to apply and click OK.

Do it!

C-5: Creating a bar with custom links

Here's how	Here's why
1 Open Recipes.htm	
2 Place the insertion point at the very bottom of the page	(Below the copyright statement.)
3 Choose **Insert**, **Navigation...**	
Under Component type, verify that Link Bars is selected	
Under Choose a bar type, verify that Bar with custom links is selected	
Click **Next**	
4 Verify that the indicated option is selected	Use Page's Theme
	To prepare to add the links in the default style of the Web page.
Click **Next**	
5 Verify that the indicated option is selected	In this orientation, links are arranged horizontally.
Click **Finish**	To open the Create New Link Bar dialog box.
6 In the Name box, enter **Recipe link**	
Click **OK**	To open the Link Bar Properties dialog box.

7 Click **Add link**	To open the Add to Link Bar dialog box.
Under Link to, select **Existing File or Web Page**	
From the list of files, select **Recipe1.htm**	
Click **OK**	The file is added to the Links list.
Click Add link and select Recipe2.htm from the list of files	To add Recipe2.htm to the Links list.
8 Click **OK**	The links are created. You can also see an "add link" hyperlink. You can click on this to add more links to the bar.
Save and close the page	
	The navigation structure of the new custom links bar, Recipe link, is automatically created in the Navigation view.

Page banners

Explanation

If you want to add titles to multiple pages on a Web site, you can create a page banner inside a shared border. Page banners can be images or text that you can format. To use a page banner to display the title of a Web page, you must first create the navigation structure for your Web site. If you don't add a page to the navigation structure, the title in the page banner won't be visible. The title in the page banner is taken from the title in Navigation view. If you change the title for a page, the text in the page banner automatically updates accordingly. To create a page banner:

1 Place the insertion point where you want the banner.

2 Choose Insert, Page Banner to open the Page Banner Properties dialog box.

3 Under Properties, select Text, if you want to display the title of the page.

4 In the Page banner text box, the title of the current page appears if the page is added to the navigation structure. Edit the text to display your desired page title.

Do it!

C-6:   Creating and modifying a page banner

Here's how	Here's why
1 Open Feedback.htm	You want to add this page to the navigation structure and create a page banner.
2 Place the insertion point at the very bottom of the page	
3 Choose **Insert, Page Banner...**	To open the Page Banner Properties dialog box.
4 Under Properties, select **Text**	The Page banner text box isn't available yet, because the page hasn't been added to the navigation structure.
Click **OK**	
5 Observe the page	
[Add this page to the navigation structure to display a page banner here]	
	A message appears, indicating that you need to add the page to the navigation structure.
6 Switch to Navigation view	Choose View, Navigation.
Add Feedback.htm to the navigation structure below the home page	
7 Choose View, Page	To switch to Page view. The title of the page appears in the page banner area.
8 Click Feedback	Feedback
	To select the page banner.
Choose **Format, Properties**	To open the Page Banner Properties dialog box. The Page banner text box is now available.
9 Edit the Page banner text box to read **feedback**	This text serves as the page banner.
Click **OK**	The banner text updates.
10 Save your changes	

Navigational elements in page banners

Explanation
You can insert a navigation bar in a page banner. If you create the banner within shared borders, the navigation bar inserted in the banner appears on all pages. To add navigation to a page banner:

1 Select the page banner text and choose Insert, Navigation to open the Insert Web Component dialog box.

2 Under Choose a bar type, select Bar based on navigation structure.

3 Click Next to move to the next dialog box, select a bar style and orientation, and click Finish to open the Link Bar Properties dialog box.

4 Select Child pages under Home.

5 Check Home page.

6 Click OK.

Do it!

C-7: Adding navigational elements to page banners

Here's how	Here's why
1 Verify that the page banner text is selected	
2 Choose **Insert, Navigation...**	To open the Insert Web Component dialog box. Under Component type, Link Bars is selected.
3 Under Choose a bar type, select **Bar based on navigation structure**	
Click **Next**	
Click **Next** again	
Click **Finish**	To open the Link Bar Properties dialog box.
4 Select **Child pages under Home**	
Check **Home page**	
Click **OK**	
5 Observe the page	A navigation bar appears in place of the banner. The banner text also appears but isn't a hyperlink, because it references the current page.
6 Save and close the page	

Topic D: Renaming pages

Explanation

Most Web sites contain a large number of hyperlinks. The task of updating hyperlinks to reflect changes to file names can be time-consuming and tedious if each hyperlink has to be updated individually. FrontPage makes this task easy by automatically updating hyperlinks to reflect changes to file names.

Updating hyperlinks

When you rename or delete a file on a Web site, FrontPage asks you to update the hyperlinks to that file. If you don't update your hyperlinks, any links to that renamed or deleted file are broken, which detracts from the usability and perceived professionalism of your Web site.

Do it!

D-1: Updating hyperlinks

Here's how	Here's why
1 Switch to Folders view	
2 Right-click **Products.htm**	To display the shortcut menu.
Choose **Rename**	
3 Edit the name to read **Productlist.htm**	
Press (↵ ENTER)	A message box appears, prompting you to update the hyperlinks to this page.
Click **Yes**	To update the hyperlinks and rename the page.
4 Maximize your browser	Index.htm, the home page for Outlander Spices, should be open.
Refresh the page	Choose View, Refresh.
5 Point to the **Products** link	(On the left side of the page.) The pointer changes to a hand.
Observe the status bar	The link points to Productlist.htm.
6 Click **Products**	To open the Productlist.htm page.
7 Close your browser	
8 Close the Web site	If prompted to save your changes, click Yes.

Unit summary: Hyperlinks

Topic A
In this topic, you learned how to create **links between pages on a Web site**. You learned that you can create links to an external Web site by providing the URL of the Web site. You learned how to test hyperlinks by using the **Preview tab** and **Design view**. You also leaned how to create and link to a **bookmark**.

Topic B
Then, you learned how to **link to an external Web site**. You also learned how to create an **email link** that opens a user's email program.

Topic C
In this topic, you learned how to create a **navigation structure** and insert a **navigation bar**. Then you learned how to create a **shared border**, a **bar with custom links**, and **page banners**. You also learned how to insert a navigation bar in a shared border and add navigational elements to page banners.

Topic D
Finally, you learned how to **update hyperlinks** to reflect changes to file names.

Independent practice activity

1 Open the Hyperlinks Practice Web site.

2 Open index.htm.

3 Make the text **Order Online** a link to Orderonline.htm (the text is on the left-side of the page).

4 Test the hyperlink, and then close the Orderonline.htm page.

5 On index.htm, make the text "Contact Us" an email link to **info@outlanderspices.com**.

6 Save your changes.

7 Create a navigation structure, as shown in Exhibit 3-3.

8 Create a navigation bar at the bottom of the Locations.htm page. This navigation bar should appear in all pages in the Web site. (Hint: You need to add a shared border first.)

9 Close all open pages.

10 Change the name of the Orderonline.htm to Orderpage.htm and update the hyperlinks.

11 Save and close the Web site.

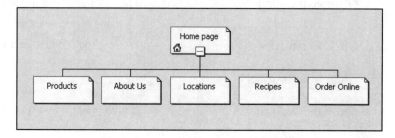

Exhibit 3-3: The navigation structure for step 9 of the Independent practice activity

Review questions

1 When inserting hyperlinks in Design view, which command can be used to test the link?

2   Which of the following links are used to activate a user's e-mail application and create a new e-mail form set to a specific address?

   A Internal

   B External

   C Mailto

   D Address

3 What is the difference between bookmarks and hyperlinks?

4 What is the purpose of creating shared borders?

5 How do you test a navigation bar in a Web browser?

Unit 4

Images

Unit time: 50 minutes

Complete this unit and you'll know how to:

A Add images to a Web page, modify and edit an image, and add an image to a bulleted list.

B Create and modify a photo gallery.

C Use images as hyperlinks and add hotspots to an image.

Topic A: Images

Explanation

You can add images to your Web pages to illustrate products and ideas or to catch the user's eye. You can also customize the appearance of a page by aligning your images, formatting text around them, and adding images as list bullets.

Images in Web pages

Images are important components of Web design. Company logos are typically images, and most Web sites have standard corporate or organizational logos that are consistent on every page of their site. You can insert various types of image files into your Web pages. The most commonly used image formats are JPG and GIF files. JPG images are typically used for photographic images that contain many colors, and GIF images are typically used for logos and image-based text.

To add an image, click the Insert Picture From File button on the Standard toolbar to open the Picture dialog box. Select the image you want to insert and click Insert.

Do it!

A-1: Inserting an image

Here's how	Here's why
1 Open the New Spices Web site	(From the current unit folder.)
2 Open Locations.htm	
Place the insertion point as shown	
3 Click [icon]	(The Insert Picture From File button is on the Standard toolbar.) To open the Picture dialog box.
Navigate to the images folder of the New Spices Web site	
Select **usa-map.gif**	
Click **Insert**	The map appears on the page. By default, it's aligned to the left.
4 Observe the HTML code	The IMG tag embeds the image. The SRC attribute specifies the name of the file and the path to its location.
Switch to Design view	
5 Save the page	

Aligning and resizing images

Explanation   You can align an image to the left, center, or right side of a page. To do so, select the image and click one of the three alignment buttons on the Formatting toolbar. (You can't justify an image, so the justify alignment button is disabled when you select an image.) You can also resize the image by dragging the sizing handle and by using Picture Actions.

Do it!   ### A-2:   Aligning and resizing an image

Here's how	Here's why
1 Click the map	To select it. If the pictures toolbar appears, close it.
Click ☰	To center the image.
2 Choose **View**, **Ruler and Grid**, **Show Ruler**	To display the ruler.
Place your cursor over the bottom-right sizing handle	Point, but don't click yet.
Note that the ruler reads 600	
3 Drag the sizing handle until the reading on the ruler is 650	The Picture Actions smart tag appears.
Click the arrow as shown	
In the list, verify that **Only Modify Size Attributes** is selected	To apply the modified size attributes, width, and height.
Hide the ruler	
4 Save and close the page	

Editing images

Explanation

You can edit images from within the FrontPage application. Microsoft Office Picture Manager, an extension of Microsoft Office 2003, is the default image editing application for FrontPage 2003.

To edit an image:

1 Right-click the image and choose Open With, Microsoft Office Picture Manager to open the image.
2 Make changes to the image by using the Edit Pictures task pane.
3 Choose File, Exit to close Microsoft Office Picture Manager and return to FrontPage.

Do it!

A-3: Editing an image

Here's how	Here's why
1 Open Products.htm	
2 Right-click the image of Cinnamon	A shortcut menu appears.
Choose **Open With, Microsoft Office Picture Manager**	The Microsoft Office Picture Manager window opens with the image already open.
3 Observe the options in the Edit Pictures task pane	
Click **Brightness and Contrast**	To open the Brightness and Contrast task pane.
Under Brightness and contrast settings, drag the Brightness bar to **12**	
Drag the Contrast bar to **24**	

4 Click **Back to Edit Pictures**

   Click 🖫   To save your changes.

5 Choose **File**, **Exit**   To close Microsoft Office Picture Manager and go back to the Microsoft FrontPage window.

6 Click **Preview**

   Observe the image   The image appears brighter. The changes made in Microsoft Office Picture Manager are reflected in FrontPage.

7 Close the page

Formatting text around images

Explanation

When you add an image to a page, any text around the image appears by default at the bottom of the image. You can align the text around an image, so that it appears at the top, bottom, or center of the image. Exhibit 4-1 is an example of text aligned to the top of an image.

To align text around an image:

1 Select the image.

2 Choose Format, Properties to open the Picture Properties dialog box.

3 Verify that the Appearance tab is activated.

4 Specify the alignment and spacing options you want.

5 Click OK.

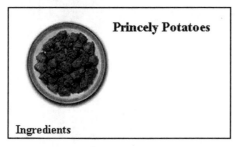

Exhibit 4-1: An image with text aligned to its top

Exhibit 4-2: The same image and text with extra spacing

Do it!   ## A-4:   Formatting text around an image

Here's how	Here's why
1 Open Recipe.htm	
Select the indicated image	
	By default, text next to an image is aligned to the bottom of the image.
2 Choose **Format**, **Properties**	To open the Picture Properties dialog box.
Verify that the Appearance tab is activated	
Under Layout, from the Alignment dropdown list, select **Texttop**	
Click **OK**	The text is now aligned to the top of the image, as shown in Exhibit 4-1.
3 Observe the HTML code	The ALIGN attribute of the IMG tag indicates that the text is top-aligned.
Switch to Design view	
4 Open the Picture Properties dialog box	(Select the image and choose Format, Properties.) To prepare to set horizontal spacing between the text and the image.
In the Horizontal spacing box, enter **30**	
Click **OK**	There are now 30 pixels of horizontal space around both sides of the image, as shown in Exhibit 4-2.
5 Observe the HTML code	The HSPACE attribute specifies the amount of horizontal spacing.
Switch to Design view	
6 Save and close the page	

Tracing images

Explanation

A common Web design technique is to create a *tracing image*. Many designers prefer to start a new design initiative by creating one large image of the entire design concept, as it will appear in a browser. Starting with an image makes it faster and easier to establish a design, get feedback from others, and make modifications.

Once you have established a design you're happy with, you can use the image within FrontPage as a guide, over which you can "trace" as you build your HTML pages. The Tracing Image feature also lets you control the opacity of the tracing image.

To insert a tracing image:

1 Choose View, Tracing Image, Configure to open the Tracing Image dialog box, as shown in Exhibit 4-3.

2 Click Browse. From the Look in list, select the picture you want.

3 Click Insert.

4 Click OK.

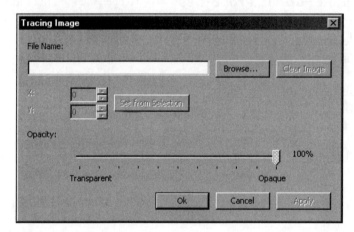

Exhibit 4-3: The Tracing Image dialog box

Do it!   **A-5:   Tracing an image**

Here's how	Here's why
1 Create a new page	
2 Choose **View**, **Tracing Image**, **Configure...**	To open the Tracing Image dialog box.
Click **Browse**	To open the Picture dialog box.
In the Look in list, navigate to the New Spices folder	You'll select an image to trace.
Select **Tracing.gif**	You'll construct a Web page based on the design in this image.
Click **Insert**	
3 Drag the Opacity bar to **70%**	
Click **Ok**	The selected image appears in the page. Note that the image appears faded, to make it easy to trace over.
4 Choose **Insert, Picture, From File...**	To insert the Top_image.jpg image from the images folder of the New Spices folder.
In the Look in box, verify that New Spices appears	
Double-click the **images** folder	
Insert **Top_image.jpg**	Select it and click Insert.
Click **Preview**	Only the newly added image appears. The tracing image is visible only in Design view.
5 Switch to Design view	
6 Place the insertion point as shown	
Type **Home**	
7 Click **Preview**	The text appears on the page.
8 Save the page as **Tracing.htm**, and close it	

Using images as bullets

Explanation

If you want to customize your lists and make them a bit more eye-catching, you can use images as your list item bullets. To use images as list bullets:

1 Select the list and choose Format, Bullets and Numbering to display the List Properties dialog box.

2 Click the Picture Bullets tab.

3 Click Browse.

4 From the list, select the picture you want.

5 Click OK to insert the image in the list.

> ► Almonds, blanched peeled and sliced 3 tbsp
> ► **Outlander Spices** Cinnamon powder 1 ½ tsp
> ► **Outlander Spices** Nutmeg powder   1 ½ tsp
> ► **Outlander Spices** Coriander powder 1 ½ tsp
> ► **Outlander Spices** Red chilli powder   3 tsp
> ► Oil 1/2cup
> ► Onions chopped 1/2cup
> ► Ginger paste 2 tsp
> ► Garlic paste 2 tsp

Exhibit 4-4: Images as list bullets

Do it!   **A-6:   Using an image as list bullets**

Here's how	Here's why
1 Open Recipe.htm	

Select the entire list

- Almonds, blanched peeled and sliced 3 tbsp
- **Outlander Spices** Cinnamon powder 1 ½ tsp
- **Outlander Spices** Nutmeg powder   1 ½ tsp
- **Outlander Spices** Coriander powder 1 ½ tsp
- **Outlander Spices** Red chili powder   3 tsp
- Oil 1/2cup
- Onions chopped 1/2cup
- Ginger paste 2 tsp
- Garlic paste 2 tsp

Here's how	Here's why
2 Choose **Format**, **Bullets and Numbering...**	The List Properties dialog box appears.

Click the **Picture Bullets** tab

Click **Browse**

Select **Bullet.gif** from the images folder in the New Spices folder

Click **Open**

3 Click **OK**	The image is applied as the bullet for each list item, as shown in Exhibit 4-4.

Deselect the text

4 Save and close the page

Topic B: Photo galleries

Explanation

If you want a collection of pictures arranged in a specific layout on a page, you can create a photo gallery. With a photo gallery, you can arrange pictures on one page or across multiple pages, like a photo album. FrontPage also makes it easy to modify an existing photo gallery.

Creating photo galleries

To create a photo gallery, choose Insert, Picture, New Photo Gallery to open the Photo Gallery Properties dialog box, as shown in Exhibit 4-5. Add the pictures you want to display in the photo gallery, select a layout, and click OK.

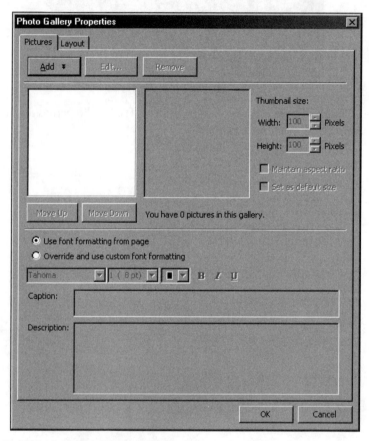

Exhibit 4-5: The Photo Gallery Properties dialog box

Do it!

B-1: Creating a photo gallery

Here's how	Here's why
1 Create a new normal page	To prepare to create a photo gallery.
Save the page as **SpiceGallery.htm**	
Close the task pane	(If necessary.)

2 Choose **Insert**, **Picture**, **New Photo Gallery...**	To open the Photo Gallery Properties dialog box. By default, the Pictures tab is activated.
3 Click **Add**	A menu appears.
Choose **Pictures from Files...**	The File Open dialog box appears.
4 Select **Cinnamon.gif**	To prepare to add this image to the photo gallery.
Click **Open**	Cinnamon.gif is added to the list of file names.
5 In the Caption box, enter **Cinnamon**	The name appears along with the image in the photo gallery.
6 Click **Add** and choose **Pictures from Files**	
From the list, select **Cloves.gif** and click **Open**	To add Cloves.gif to the photo gallery.
Verify that Cloves.gif is selected	
In the Caption box, enter **Cloves**	
7 Add **Coriander.gif**, **Cumin.gif**, **Nutmeg.gif**, and **Pepper.gif** to the photo gallery	The images appear in the list.
Select the image and enter the name in the Caption box	Use the names of each spice as the image captions.
8 Click the **Layout** tab	
9 Under Choose a layout, select **Vertical Layout**	A preview of the layout appears.
Observe the Number of pictures per row list	3 is the default. This indicates that the photo gallery contains three pictures per row.
10 Click **OK**	The images appear arranged in the photo gallery. The captions are displayed to the right side of their associated images.
Save the page	

Modifying photo galleries

Explanation

FrontPage makes it easy to modify photo galleries by changing the order of the images, the gallery layout, or the placement of the captions. You can also remove images from the gallery.

To modify a photo gallery, right-click anywhere on the photo gallery and choose Photo Gallery Properties to open the Photo Gallery Properties dialog box. Make the desired changes and click OK.

Do it!

B-2: Modifying a photo gallery

Here's how	Here's why
1 Right-click the photo gallery	
Choose **Photo Gallery Properties**	To open the Photo Gallery Properties dialog box.
2 Select **Pepper.gif**	
Click **Remove**	Pepper.gif no longer appears in the list.
3 Select **Nutmeg.gif**	(If it's not already selected.) To prepare to make this the first image in the gallery.
Click **Move Up** four times	Nutmeg.gif moves up in the list.
4 Verify that Nutmeg.gif is selected	
In the Caption box, select **Nutmeg**	To prepare to change the formatting of the caption.
5 Select **Override and use custom font formatting**	Formatting options are displayed.
6 From the font list, select **Arial**	
From the Color palette, select a color	

7 Click the **Layout** tab

From the Number of pictures per row list, select **2**

(Scroll up, if necessary.) To arrange the pictures two per row.

Click **OK**

Deselect the photo gallery

Nutmeg.gif appears as the first image in the gallery. The caption, Nutmeg, is formatted differently. Also, Pepper.gif is no longer in the gallery, and only two pictures appear in each row.

8 Save and close the page

Topic C: Image links

Explanation

With FrontPage, it's easy to set images as hyperlinks. You can also create multiple links within a single image. Multiple links are helpful if you want to use an image as a navigational tool or, like a bookmark, to jump to different sections of a page.

Using images as hyperlinks

To make an image a hyperlink, select the image and choose Insert, Hyperlink. In the Insert Hyperlink dialog box, select the page you want to link to and click OK.

Do it!

C-1: Creating an image link

Here's how	Here's why
1 Open index.htm	
2 Select the indicated image	The Market leader in quality spices
3 Open the Insert Hyperlink dialog box	
Select **Existing File or Web Page**	
From the list, select **AboutUs.htm**	
Click **OK**	
4 Switch to Preview	
Point to the image	The pointer changes to a hand, indicating that the image is a link.
Click the image	AboutUs.htm appears.
Switch to Design view	To return to index.htm.
5 Save and close the page	

Hotspots in images

Explanation

You can link various parts of an image to different pages or different sections of a page by creating a *hotspot*, an informal name for a link within an image. For example, you can create hotspots on a map of the United States so that each state links to a different page. An image containing hotspots is called an *image map*.

To create a hotspot:

1 Select the image.

2 On the Pictures toolbar, click the shape that best fits the hotspot region you want to create. You can choose a rectangle, a polygon, or a circle.

3 Draw the shape around the desired part of the image. When you complete the shape, the Insert Hyperlink dialog box opens.

4 Select the page, e-mail address, or URL of the Web site you want to link to and click OK.

Do it!

C-2: Creating a hotspot

Here's how	Here's why
1 Open Locations.htm	(This page contains an image of the United States.) To prepare to create hotspot areas around specific states, so that you can link to information related to those states.
2 Select the map	
3 Display the Pictures toolbar	(If necessary.) Choose View, Toolbars, Pictures.
Click ▢	(The Rectangular Hotspot button is on the Pictures toolbar.) To create a rectangular hotspot.
4 Point to the image as shown	The pointer takes the shape of a pencil.
Drag to create a rectangle as shown	To define a rectangular hotspot. The Insert Hyperlink dialog box appears.
5 Click **Bookmark**	To open the Select Place in Document dialog box.
From the list, select **Washington**	To create a hyperlink to a bookmark.
Click **OK**	
Click **OK**	To create the link and close the Insert Hyperlink dialog box.

6 Click 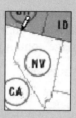 (The Polygonal Hotspot button is on the Pictures toolbar.) To create a polygonal hotspot.

Point to the map as shown

The pointer takes the shape of a pencil. When you click, you define the first corner of the polygon.

Click as shown

Click at the indicated position

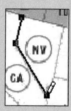

Click at the indicated position

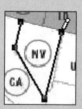

Click at the indicated position

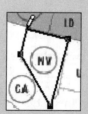

To create the third edge.

Create the fourth edge

To close the polygon and open the Insert Hyperlink dialog box.

7   Click the Bookmark button

From the Select Place in
Document dialog box, select
Nevada and click **OK**

To link the hotspot to the bookmark Nevada

Click **OK**

8   Switch to Preview

9   Point to the Washington hotspot

The pointer takes the shape of a hand, indicating
a link.

10   Test the hotspot

To move to the linked location. The hotspot is
linked to a section within the same page.

Scroll up

11   Test the Nevada hotspot

Switch to Design view

Close the Pictures toolbar

12   Save and close the page

Close the Web site

Unit summary: Images

Topic A   In this topic, you learned how to **embed** an image and **align** it in a page. You also learned that you can **edit images** by using the Microsoft Office Picture Manager. In addition, you learned how to **format text around an image** and use **images as list bullets**.

Topic B   In this topic, you learned how to create **photo galleries**. You also learned how to modify a photo gallery by changing the layout and captions of images.

Topic C   Finally, you learned how to create **image links**. You also learned how to add **hotspots** in an image map. You learned that you can create hotspots of different shapes by using the different hotspot buttons on the Pictures toolbar.

Independent practice activity

1 Open the Images Practice Web site.

2 Open **Recipe.htm**.

3 Insert **Recipe2.jpg** at the top of the page. (Hint: The file is in the images folder under Images Practice.)

4 Center-align the image and add the caption, "Chicken stuffed with spices," at the bottom of the image, as shown in Exhibit 4-6.

5 Align the text to the top of the image.

6 Use the image **Bullet.gif** as the bullet for the list below the text, "For the stuffing."

7 Save and close the page. (Click OK if the Save Embedded Files dialog box appears.)

8 Open **AboutUs.htm**. Link the image **home.gif** at the bottom of the page to the file index.htm.

9 Save the page.

10 Test the image link in your browser.

11 Close the browser.

12 Create a rectangular hotspot on the area shown in Exhibit 4-7. Link the hotspot to theprojectteam bookmark.

13 Save the page.

14 Test the hotspot in your browser.

15 Close your browser and the Pictures toolbar.

16 Close the Web site.

Exhibit 4-6: *The Recipe page after step 4*

Exhibit 4-7: The area to be converted to a hotspot in step 12

Review questions

1 Which of the following image format is used for photographic images that contain many colors?

A HTML

B GIF

C JPG

D HTTP

2 How do you add an image to a Web page?

3 When you add an image to a page, where does any text around the image appear by default?

A Top

B Bottom

C Left

D Right

4 What is the procedure that you would use to use images instead of round bullets in a list?

5 What type of links would you need to create if you wanted each state on a map of the United States to link to a different page?

6 Why is the Justify alignment button not available when you select an image?

Unit 5

Tables

Unit time: 45 minutes

Complete this unit, and you'll know how to:

A Insert a table, add images and text to a table, insert and delete rows and columns, insert nested tables, add captions, and copy content from one cell to multiple cells.

B Enhance the appearance of a table by changing table and cell properties and by using AutoFormat.

Topic A: Applying tables

Explanation

Tables are an effective way of presenting organized data, such as a product list or a reference table. You can also use tables as design tools, because they enable you to combine text, pictures, and white space easily into complex arrangements.

Tables

A *table* is a grid composed of rows and columns with data contained in individual cells. A *cell* is an intersection of a row and a column.

You can create a table by using a template, the Table toolbar, or the Table, Insert, Table command. Whichever method you use, all you need to do is specify how many rows and columns you want.

Do it!

A-1:   Inserting a table

Here's how	Here's why
1 Open the Tables Web site	(From the current unit folder.)
Open Locations.htm	
2 Place the insertion to the right of the links, as shown	
3 Choose **Table**, **Insert**, **Table...**	To open the Insert Table dialog box.
In the Rows box, under Size, enter **4**	
In the Columns box, verify that **2** is displayed	(2 is the default.)
Click **OK**	A table with four rows and two columns appears on the page.
4 Observe the HTML code	The TABLE tags are the primary tags that surround the rest of the text and code within a table. The sets of TR tags within the TABLE tags define the rows in the table. The sets of TD tags between the TR tags define the cells in each row.
Switch to Design view	

5 Enter **Washington**

The insertion point appears in the first cell, which is the intersection of the first row and the first column.

Press (TAB)

To move to the second cell. You can move from one cell to another by using the Tab key or by using the arrow keys.

Enter
**Shopper's Paradise, Seattle
Blue Heaven, Seattle Stop
'n Shop**

6 Save the page

Images in a table

Explanation

You insert images in table cells the same way you would anywhere else on a Web page. The table helps you to align the picture above, below, or to the left or right of other images or text. When you align an image in a table cell, the alignment is relative to the cell, rather than to the entire page.

To add an image to a table, place the insertion point in the desired cell. Open the Picture dialog box, select the picture, and click Insert.

Exhibit 5-1: The Locations page after step 7

Do it!

A-2:   Adding an image to a table

Here's how	Here's why
1 Place the insertion point as shown	
Choose **Table**, **Insert**, **Table…**	To open the Insert Table dialog box.
2 Verify that the Rows box reads 2	
In the Columns box, enter **1**	
Click **OK**	To insert a table with two rows and one column.
3 Place the insertion point in the second cell	
4 Open the Picture dialog box	
Select **usa-map.gif**	(From the images folder of the Tables Web site.)
Click **Insert**	The image now appears in the second row of the table.
5 Observe the HTML code	The IMG tag appears within the TD tags of the cell.
Switch to Design view	
6 Select the image and click the **Center** button on the Formatting toolbar	To center the image.
7 Place the insertion point in the first cell of the table	
Type **You can now purchase our products from the kiosks located in the states below.**	The page now appears, as shown in Exhibit 5-1.
8 Save the page	

The Draw Table button

Explanation

The Table toolbar contains several tools, as shown in Exhibit 5-2. You can use these tools to create and modify tables. One of these tools is the Draw Table button, which you can use to draw a table or to add cell borders to subdivide existing cells.

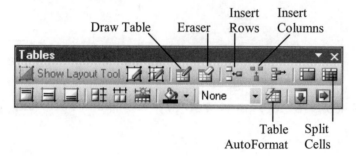

Exhibit 5-2: The Tables toolbar

Split cells

When you need to divide an existing cell into multiple cells, you can use the Draw Table button or the Split Cells command.

To subdivide an existing cell by using the Split Cells command:
1 Place the insertion point in the cell.
2 Choose Table, Split Cells to open the Split Cells dialog box.
3 In the Split Cells dialog box, select the relevant option to split the cell into rows or columns and select the number of rows or columns into which you want to split the cell.
4 Click OK.

To split an existing cell by using the Draw Table button:
1 Display the Tables toolbar and select the Draw Table button.
2 Draw a line within the cell to create a new column or row.
3 Click the Draw Table button to complete the drawing of the cell.

Do it!   ### A-3:   Using the Draw Table button

Here's how	Here's why
1 Place the insertion point at the bottom of the page, as shown	
2 Choose **View, Toolbars, Tables**	The Tables toolbar appears.
Click	(The Draw Table button is on the Tables toolbar.)
Click as shown	
	The pointer changes to a pen.
Drag as shown	
	To create the table outline.
3 Draw a line across the middle of the cell, as shown	
	To split the table into two rows.
4 In the top cell, point and draw as shown	
	To subdivide the first row.
5 Divide the second row	
6 Click	To deactivate the Draw Table tool.
7 Close the Tables toolbar	Choose View, Toolbars, Tables.
8 Save the page	

Adding rows and columns

Explanation

You can easily insert additional rows and columns to increase the capacity of a table. Here's how:

1   Place the insertion point in the row or column before or after which you want to insert a row or column.

2   Choose Table, Insert, Rows or Columns to open the Insert Rows or Columns dialog box.

3   In the dialog box, specify the number of rows or columns you want to add and whether you want to insert them before or after the location of the insertion point.

4   Click OK.

When you are in the last cell of a table, pressing Tab automatically adds a new row.

Do it!

A-4:   Inserting an additional row and column

Here's how	Here's why
1 Place the insertion point in the last cell of the table	
2 Choose **Table**, **Insert, Rows or Columns...**	To open the Insert Rows or Columns dialog box.
Verify that Rows is selected	The Number of rows box reads 1. This indicates that one row is to be added to the table.
Under Location, verify that Below selection is selected	
Click **OK**	To add a row to the table.
3 Observe the table	The table now contains three rows.
4 Place the insertion point in the last cell	
Press (TAB)	A new row is added to the table.
5 Save the page	

Deleting rows and columns

Explanation

To delete rows and columns, place the insertion point in the row or column that you want to delete. Choose Table, Select, Row or Column to select the row or column. Then, choose Table, Delete Rows or Columns.

Deleting tables

You can also delete a table completely. To do this, select the table by choosing Table, Select, Table. Then choose Table, Delete Cells.

Do it!

A-5: Deleting a row and column

Here's how	Here's why
1 Place the insertion point in the last row	If necessary.
2 Choose **Table, Select, Row**	
3 Choose **Table, Delete Rows**	To delete the selected row.
Switch to Design view	
4 Place the insertion point in the first cell of the table	
Choose **Table, Select, Column**	To select the first column.
5 Choose **Table, Delete Columns**	To delete the first column.
6 Choose **Table, Select, Table**	To select the entire table.
Choose **Table, Delete Cells**	To delete the entire table.
7 Select the table below the map	You'll delete the second table.
Choose **Table, Delete Cells**	To delete the table.
8 Save the page	

Nested tables

Explanation

A common design technique is to use nested tables to achieve a desired content layout. A nested table is simply a table that's inserted into a cell of another table. This technique often provides more options for organizing and arranging information.

To create a nested table, place the insertion point in the table cell where you want to insert the new table, and then choose Table, Insert, Table.

Washington	Shopper's Paradise, Seattle Blue Heaven, Seattle Stop 'n Shop
Oregon	Shopper's Paradise, Portland
Nevada	Plaza Givo, Las Vegas
California	Shopper's Paradise, Los Angeles

Exhibit 5-3: The nested table after step 7

Do it!

A-6: Inserting a nested table

Here's how	Here's why
1 Place the insertion point in the cell to the right of the map	You'll add a new row.
Press (IAB)	To add a new row.
2 Choose **Table, Insert, Table...**	
3 In the Rows box, enter **4**	(Use the default 2 columns.) You want the table to consist of 4 rows and 2 columns.
Under Layout, from the Alignment list, select **Center**	
Click **OK**	The table appears in the page.
4 Observe the HTML code	You can see that another TABLE tag is added within the first TABLE tag.
Switch to Design view	

5   In the first cell, enter
Washington

Press (TAB)

Enter **Shopper's Paradise**,
Seattle Blue Heaven,
Seattle Stop 'n Shop,
Tacoma Treasure,
Redmond

Press (TAB)

Enter **Oregon**

6   Enter the remaining text   As shown in Exhibit 5-3.

7   Save the page

Table captions

You can easily add a caption to a table. A *caption* is a title for the table that appears at the top of the table.

To insert a caption, place the insertion point anywhere inside the table and choose Table, Insert, Caption. The insertion point appears at the top center of the table. You can then enter your caption.

A-7: Adding a caption to a table

Here's how	Here's why
1 Place the insertion point inside the nested table	If necessary.
2 Choose **Table**, **Insert**, **Caption**	The insertion point appears at the top of the table.
3 Type **Outlander Spices retail outlets**	You can format the caption the same as you would any other text on the Web page.
4 Save and close the page	

Repetitive information

Explanation   If you need to enter repetitive information in the cells of a table, FrontPage can do the work for you. For example, let's say you want to enter the details of various retail outlets of Outlander Spices. The names of the stores are the same, while the states and the cities are different. In such a situation, you need not type the same store name multiple times.

Enter the information in the first row or column and select the rows or columns where you want to have the same information. Then, choose Table, Fill, Down or Right as the case may be.

Washington	Shopper's Paradise
Oregon	
California	

Exhibit 5-4: The table after step 2

Do it!   ## A-8:   Copying content from one cell to multiple cells

Here's how	Here's why
1 Open a new page	
2 Insert a table of three rows and two columns	
Enter the text in the table	As shown in Exhibit 5-4.
3 Place the insertion point anywhere in the second column	
Choose **Table**, **Select**, **Column**	To select the column.
4 Choose **Table**, **Fill**, **Down**	The text "Shopper's Paradise" is copied into the other two cells.
5 Save the page as **Stores.htm** and close it	

Topic B: Formatting tables

Explanation

FrontPage makes it easy to format tables. You can set the properties for an entire table or for individual cells. FrontPage also helps you change the color of the table, so that it matches the design of your Web page.

Table properties

Some properties apply to an entire table, including border style, cell padding, and background image. You can use the Table, Table Properties, Table command to display the Table Properties dialog box. You can set these properties in Table Properties dialog box, as shown in Exhibit 5-5.

In this dialog box, you can use the Layout options to specify the alignment of the table in the Web page, the space between two consecutive cells (cell spacing), the space between the cell border and the text in the cell (cell padding), the width, and the height of the table. By using the Borders options, you can specify the size and color of the table borders. Finally, you can use the Background options to specify a background color or image for the table.

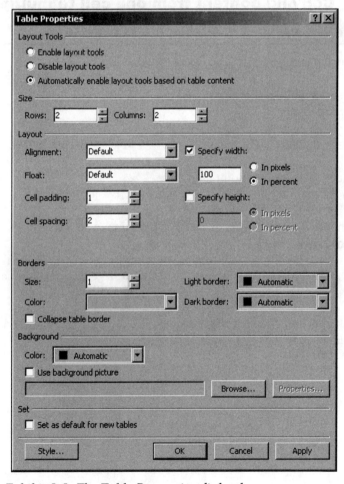

Exhibit 5-5: The Table Properties dialog box

Do it!

B-1:   Modifying table properties

Here's how	Here's why
1 Open Locations.htm	
Place the insertion point in the first table	You can now purchase
2 Choose **Table**, **Table Properties**, **Table**	To open the Table Properties dialog box.
Under Borders, in the Size box, enter **0**	To remove the borders from the page.
Under Layout, in the Cell padding box, enter **0**	To remove the space between the cell border and text in the cell. Now, the text in the table appears closer to the border.
In the Cell spacing box, enter **0**	To remove the space between the cells. Now, the adjacent cell borders merge.
Click **OK**	
3 Observe the HTML code	The attributes enclosed within the TABLE tags indicate that the border size, cell spacing, and cell padding are 0.
Switch to Design view	
4 Place the insertion point in the nested table	The nested table is below the map.
Right-click and choose **Table Properties**	To open the Table Properties dialog box.
Under Borders, from the Color list, select a color	
Under Background, from the Color list, select the color indicated here	
Click **OK**	To apply the changes. The background color of the nested table has changed to a pale yellow, and the border color has changed.
5 Save the page	

Cell properties

Explanation

You can change the properties of a specific cell to make the information in that cell stand out. You can also modify the cell properties, such as height or width, so that the size of the cell is more suitable for its contents. To change the properties of a cell, place the insertion point in the cell and choose Table, Table Properties, Cell. The Cell Properties dialog box appears, as shown in Exhibit 5-6.

Cell properties include background images or colors, borders, height, and width. You can use the Layout options in the Cell Properties dialog box to specify the horizontal and vertical alignment of text within a table cell. You can use the other options to span a cell across more than one row or column, specify the width and the height, and create header cells. The Borders and Background options are similar to those of the Table Properties dialog box.

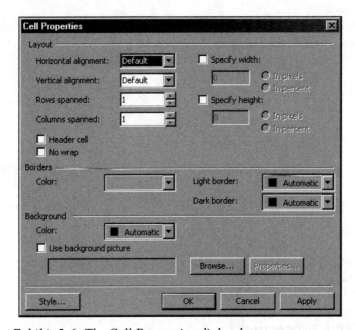

Exhibit 5-6: The Cell Properties dialog box

Do it! **B-2: Modifying cell properties**

Here's how	Here's why
1 Place the insertion point in the first cell with text in the first table	
2 Choose **Table**, **Table Properties, Cell**	To open the Cell Properties dialog box.
3 Under Layout, from the Horizontal alignment list, select **Center**	
4 Under Background, from the Color list, select the color indicated here	
Click **OK**	The row now has a pale yellow background and the text is aligned to the center of the cell
5 Save the page	

Table AutoFormat

Explanation

You can also insert a table in a Web page and apply a predefined format to it. With FrontPage's AutoFormat, you can choose a predefined format, which can save time and help you maintain a consistent format for the tables in your Web site.

To apply an AutoFormat:

1 Place the insertion point anywhere in the table.

2 Choose Table, Table AutoFormat to open the Table AutoFormat dialog box, as shown in Exhibit 5-7.

3 From the list of available formats, select the style you want to apply.

4 Under Formats to Apply, select the options you want to apply to the table.

5 Under Apply special formats, select the parts of the table to which you want to apply the formatting.

6 Click OK.

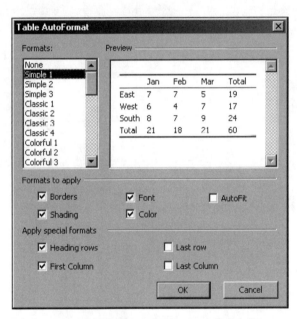

Exhibit 5-7: The Table AutoFormat dialog box

Do it!   **B-3:   Applying predefined table formats**

Here's how	Here's why
1 Observe the nested table	Scroll down. The table contains the names of states and the stores in the states where Outlander Spices have retail outlets. The table isn't formatted yet.
2 Place the insertion point in the first row	
Choose **Table**, **Insert**, **Rows or Columns...**	To open the Insert Rows or Columns dialog box. You want to insert a row at the top to add the headings for the columns.
3 Verify that Rows is selected	
Under Location, select **Above selection**	
Click **OK**	A blank row is inserted at the top of the table.
4 In the first row, first column, enter **State**	This is the heading for the first column.
Press TAB	
Enter **Retail Outlets**	
5 Choose **Table**, **Table AutoFormat...**	To open the Table AutoFormat dialog box.
6 From the Formats list, select **Classic 2**	The style appears in the Preview.
Under Apply special formats, Clear **First Column**	
Click **OK**	The table is now formatted according to the style you selected.
7 Save and close the page	
Close the Web site	

Unit summary: Tables

Topic A

In this topic, you learned how to **insert a table** and **add images** to it. You also learned to use the **Draw Table button** to **split cells**, and you learned how to **add rows** and **columns** to a table. Then you learned how to **delete** rows and columns, insert **nested tables**, and add **captions** to tables. You also learned how to copy content from one cell to multiple cells.

Topic B

Finally, you learned how to format tables. You learned how to change **table properties**, such as table borders and cell padding and spacing, by using the Table Properties dialog box. You also learned how to change **cell properties**, such as background color and alignment. Then, you learned how to **auto-format** a table by using the Table AutoFormat dialog box.

Independent practice activity

1 Open the Tables Practice Web site.

2 Create a blank page.

3 Save the page as **Products.htm**.

4 Create a table with 2 rows and 2 columns.

5 Add Cloves.gif and Cumin.gif, as shown in Exhibit 5-8. (Hint: the files are in the images folder under Tables Practice.)

6 Add text for Cloves and Cumin, as shown in Exhibit 5-8.

7 Add an additional row and enter the text for Cinnamon, as shown in Exhibit 5-8. Also add the Cinnamon.gif image.

8 Remove the borders from the table.

9 Change the cell padding and spacing to **2**. Compare the table with the table in Exhibit 5-8.

10 Save the page. (Save the embedded files also.)

11 Close the Web site.

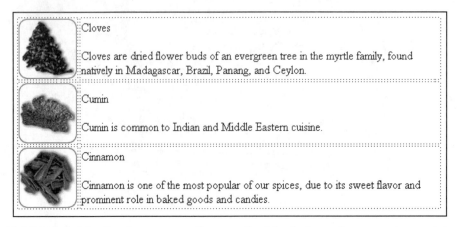

Exhibit 5-8: The Products page after step 8 of the independent practice activity

Review questions

1 Name one method that can be used to create a table.

2 When examining the HTML code for a table, what is the difference between the TR and TD tags?

3 Which of the following table properties settings is used to specify the amount of space between the cell border and the text in the cell?

   A Float

   B Cell spacing

   C Cell padding

   D Gutter

4 What is the function of the Table, Split Cells command?

5 Which of the following Layout options in the Cell Properties dialog box is used to span a cell across more than one column?

   A Rows spanned

   B Columns spanned

   C No wrap

   D Horizontal alignment

6 What is the procedure to apply a pre-defined table format to your table?

Unit 6
Enhancing Web pages

Unit time: 40 minutes

Complete this unit and you'll know how to:

A Set page properties, add a background image to a Web page, and remove a background image.

B Apply a theme to a Web site and customize an existing theme.

Topic A: Page properties

Explanation

Page properties, such as text color, margins, and background color, play a large role in the overall look and feel of a Web page. You can set these properties by using the Page Properties dialog box. When you set background color or background image, you must make sure that the color doesn't detract from the readability of the text.

Page properties

The Page Properties dialog box provides several tabs with which you can change different aspects of the page design, including the background color, margins, and page title.

Hyperlink rollover effects

You can add rollover effects to a hyperlink, so that when a user points to a text link, the style changes to reinforce the active link visually. This effect applies to all the hyperlinks on the page, rather than to individual hyperlinks.

To set rollover effects, choose File, Properties to open the Page Properties dialog box. Click the Advanced tab. Check Enable hyperlink rollover effects and click Rollover style. Select the font options and click OK. Close the Page Properties dialog box and preview the page to view the results.

Do it!

A-1: Setting page properties

Here's how	Here's why
1 Open the Enhancing Web site	(From the current unit folder.)
Open index.htm	
2 Switch to Preview	
Point to the hyperlinks	(At the left side of the page.) Notice that the color of the hyperlinks changes to maroon. You want to apply rollover effects to these hyperlinks.
3 Switch to Design view	
4 Choose **File**, **Properties…**	To open the Page Properties dialog box. The General tab is active. The Title box displays the title of the page.
5 Edit the Title box to read **Outlander Spices – Home Page**	To change the title of the page.

6 Click the **Formatting** tab

    Under Colors, from the Background list, select **Automatic**   To clear the current page background color.

7 Click the **Advanced** tab

    Under Styles, check **Enable hyperlink rollover effects**

    Click **Rollover style**   To open the Font dialog box. The current color setting is red.

    Under Effects, check **All caps**   The hyperlinks appear in capital letters when moused over.

    Click **OK**   To close the Font dialog box.

    Click **OK** again   To close the Page Properties dialog box and apply the new settings.

8 Save and preview the page

    Point to the hyperlinks at the left-side of the page   The color of the hyperlink changes to red, and the hyperlinks appear as capital letters. This is a rollover effect.

    Switch to Design view

Background pictures

Explanation

You can also use the Page Properties dialog box to add and remove background pictures. To add a background picture:

1   Open the Page Properties dialog box.
2   Click the Formatting tab.
3   Check Background picture.
4   Click Browse and select a picture.
5   Click OK.

To remove a background picture, open the Page Properties dialog box. On the Background tab, clear the Background picture option, and click OK.

Do it!

A-2:   Adding and removing a background picture

Here's how	Here's why
1 Choose **File**, **Properties**	To open the Page Properties dialog box.
2 Click the **Formatting** tab	
Under Background, check **Background picture**	To make the Background picture box available.
Click **Browse**	To open the Select Background Picture dialog box.
Select **Background.gif**	(The image is in the images folder of the Enhancing Web site.) To prepare to add this image as a background image.
Click **Open**	To close the Select Background Picture dialog box. The name of the selected image appears in the Background picture box.
3 Click **OK**	The background picture appears on the page.
4 Save the page	
5 Open the Page Properties dialog box	
6 Activate the Formatting tab	
Clear **Background picture**	
Click **OK**	The page no longer has a background image.
7 Save the page	

Topic B: Themes

Explanation
You can use FrontPage to apply a set of backgrounds, images, and formats to all the pages of your site by using themes. Themes can help you establish a consistent design for all your pages.

Applying a theme to a Web site

A *theme* is a set of background and foreground images, formats, and font styles that is applied to all the pages on your site or to specific pages that you select. FrontPage provides several themes from which to choose. When you apply a theme to a Web site, all other page formatting is removed.

To apply a theme to a Web site, choose Format, Theme to open the Theme task pane. Under All available themes, select the theme that you want to apply to your Web site. Click the menu and choose Apply as default theme.

Applying a theme to individual pages

You can also apply a theme to individual pages. To apply a theme to a single page, open the page in Design view, or if you want to apply a theme to multiple pages, select the desired pages in Folders view.

Choose Format, Theme to display the Theme task pane. Select the theme you want to apply. Click the arrow next to the preview to open a menu and choose Apply to selected page(s).

Do it!

B-1: Applying a theme

Here's how	Here's why
1 Choose **Format**, **Theme...**	To display the Theme task pane.
2 Observe the options under Select a theme	Under Web site default theme, No theme appears.
Observe the options under All available themes	Scroll down, if necessary.
3 Observe the preview of the Profile theme	Scroll down.
Click the arrow next to the preview, as shown	
	To open a menu.
Choose **Apply to selected page(s)**	The theme is thus applied to the selected page only.
4 Preview the page	
Observe the HTML code	`<meta name="Microsoft Theme" content="profile 1011">`
	The code shows that a Profile theme has been applied.
Switch to Design view	
5 Save the page	

Changing themes

Explanation

You can easily remove a theme or apply a new theme to a Web site. When you remove a theme, the formatting of all the pages in your site is removed, and you can't restore the previous format. To format the page again, you need to apply a new theme or manually format the pages.

To remove or change a theme for a Web page, display the Theme task pane. Under All available themes, select No Theme. You can then apply a new theme, if necessary.

To remove or change a theme for an entire Web site, display the Theme task pane. Under All available themes, select No Theme. Then, click the arrow next to No Theme and choose Apply as the default theme from the menu. If necessary, you can apply a new theme to the Web site.

Do it!

B-2: Removing and changing a theme

Here's how	Here's why
1 Choose **Format**, **Theme**	To display the Theme task pane, if necessary.
Under All available themes, click **No Theme**	(Scroll up.) To remove the theme that's currently applied to the page.
2 From All available themes, select **Expedition**	To apply the Expedition theme to the current page.
3 Save the page	

Customizing themes

Explanation

You can modify the colors, graphics, and text styles of an existing theme. This is helpful if you want the theme to complement the existing structure and contents of your Web site.

To customize a theme:

1   Display the Themes task pane.

2   Select the theme you want to modify and open the menu.

3   Choose Customize to open the Customize Theme dialog box.

4   Click the Colors, Graphics, or Text button depending on what you want to modify.

5   After you make the changes, save the customized theme with the same or a different name.

Do it!

B-3:   Customizing a theme

Here's how	Here's why
1 Observe the hyperlink styles on the page	The hyperlinks on the left side of the page are maroon.
2 Display the Theme task pane	(If necessary.) Under Recently used themes, Expedition appears.
Click the arrow next to the preview of Expedition theme, as shown	
	To open a menu.
3 Choose **Customize...**	To open the Customize Theme dialog box.
4 Click **Colors**	To open the Customize Theme dialog box with the Color Schemes tab activated.
5 Click the **Custom** tab	
From the Item list, select **Hyperlinks**	(You can see the color of the hyperlinks in the Preview of: Expedition pane.)
From the Color list, select the dark blue color	The color of the Regular Hyperlink changes in the Preview of: Expedition pane.
Click **OK**	

6 Click **Graphics**

In the Item list, verify that
Background Picture is selected

Click **Browse**   To open the Open File dialog box.

7 From the list of files, select   (From the images folder of the Enhancing Web
Background.gif   site.)

Click **Open**   The background picture you selected appears in
                                          the Preview of: Expedition pane.

Click **OK**

8 Click **Save As**   To open the Save Theme dialog box.

Edit the Enter new theme title box
to read **My custom theme**

Click **OK**

9 Click **OK** again   To close the Customize Theme dialog box.
                                          Under All available themes, My custom theme
                                          appears.

10 Apply My custom theme to the   The color of the hyperlinks changes to blue.
page   Also, the background of the page changes.

Close the Theme task pane

11 Save and close the page

Close the Web site

Unit summary: Enhancing Web pages

Topic A

In this topic, you learned how to set **page properties**, such as **background color**. You learned that you can add **rollover effects** to hyperlinks by using the Page Properties dialog box. You also learned how to add and remove a **background picture**.

Topic B

Finally, you learned how to apply and change a **theme**. You learned that a theme is a set of graphics and format styles that gives a consistent look to your Web site. You also learned how to **customize a theme**.

Independent practice activity

1 Open the Enhancing Practice Web site.

2 Open Locations.htm.

3 Add **Background.gif** as the background image to the page.

4 Save and preview the page. (If the Save Embedded Files dialog box appears, click OK.)

5 Apply the **Compass** theme to the Web site. (Hint: Choose Apply as default theme from the menu. If a warning box appears, click Yes.)

6 Save and preview the Web site. (If Confirm Save dialog box appears, click Yes.)

7 Customize the theme, so that the color of the hyperlinks is **Black**. Save theme as **My theme**. Apply the new theme to the Locations.htm page.

8 Save the page and close the Web site.

9 Close the Theme task pane.

Review questions

1 What is the advantage of specifying a hypertext rollover effect?

2 What is the procedure used to add a background picture on your Web page?

3 What is the advantage of using themes?

4 What happens to the formatting of a Web page when you remove a theme?

5 What can you do if you want a theme to complement the existing structure and contents of your Web site?

Unit 7

Working with HTML code

Unit time: 55 minutes

Complete this unit, and you'll know how to:

A View the HTML tree structure, manipulate items by using the Quick Tag Selector, and edit tags by using the Quick Tag Editor.

B Use the IntelliSense feature, set word wrap and line numbers, customize code indentation, find matching tags, insert comments, create bookmarks, create and insert code snippets, and optimize HTML code.

Topic A: Working in Design view

Explanation

While designing a Web site in Design view, you might want to work with the HTML code for the page without changing the view. FrontPage 2003 provides features that make it easy to modify the HTML of a page directly. These features are called Quick Tag Editor and Quick Tag Selector.

HTML tree structure

You can view the HTML tree structure of a page while working in Design view. If you place the insertion point anywhere on the Web page, the Quick Tag Selector shows the HTML tree structure. The HTML tree structure shows the hierarchy of HTML tags used in the Web page up to the selected point.

Do it!

A-1:   Viewing the HTML tree structure

Here's how	Here's why
1 Open the Outlander Spices Web site	(From the current unit folder.)
Open index.htm	
2 Choose **View**, **Quick Tag Selector**	To activate the Quick Tag Selector.
3 Select the **Outlander Spices** image, as shown	
Observe the HTML tree structure	
	Note that the IMG tag is selected. The HTML tree structure indicates that the image is inside a table.
4 Place the insertion point somewhere else in the page	The HTML tree structure changes to indicate the structure around that new point.

Manipulating items by using the Quick Tag Selector

Explanation

The Quick Tag Selector helps select any HTML tagand modify it. From the Quick Tag Selector, select a specific HTML tag and open its menu. The menu contains options for performing actions, such as selecting a tag, selecting only the tag content, or editing the tag.

To select an HTML tag's contents, on the Quick Tag Selector, select the tag and click the arrow next to it. From the menu, choose Select Tag Contents. If you want to select only a tag, open the menu of the tag, and choose Select Tag. To edit the tag, choose Edit Tag from the menu.

Do it!

A-2: Manipulating items

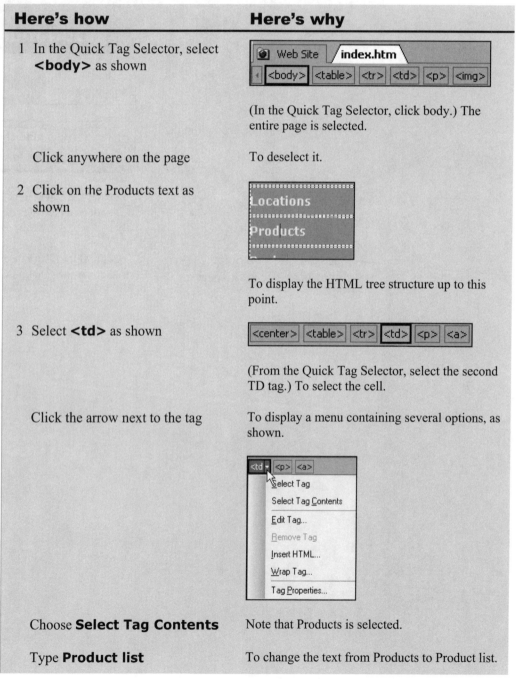

Here's how	Here's why
1 In the Quick Tag Selector, select **\<body\>** as shown	(In the Quick Tag Selector, click body.) The entire page is selected.
Click anywhere on the page	To deselect it.
2 Click on the Products text as shown	To display the HTML tree structure up to this point.
3 Select **\<td\>** as shown	(From the Quick Tag Selector, select the second TD tag.) To select the cell.
Click the arrow next to the tag	To display a menu containing several options, as shown.
Choose **Select Tag Contents**	Note that Products is selected.
Type **Product list**	To change the text from Products to Product list.

4 Click the About Us text

   Open the menu for the second TD   (In the Quick Tag Selector, click the arrow next
   tag   to the TD tag.)

   Choose **Tag Properties...**   (The Cell Properties dialog box appears.) You
                                              can now change the properties of this cell, such
                                              as layout, borders, or background.

5 Under Background, click the   To display the Color list. You want to change
   arrow next to Color   the background color of the cell.

   Select the maroon color

   Click **OK**   To apply the new color to the cell and close the
                                              Cell Properties dialog box.

   Deselect the text   The background color of the cell changes to
                                              maroon.

6 Save and close the page

The Quick Tag Editor

Explanation

The Quick Tag Editor helps you create and edit HTML tags within the Design view. For example, you can change the width of a table cell or any other properties of a table by using the Quick Tag Editor without moving out of the Design view.

To use the Quick Tag Editor:

1   In the Quick Tag Selector, select the tag.
2   Click the arrow next to the tag to display the menu.
3   From the menu, choose Edit Tag.
4   After editing the tag, click the Enter button.

Exhibit 7-1: The Quick Tag Editor after step 3

Do it!

A-3:   Editing tags by using the Quick Tag Editor

Here's how	Here's why
1 Create a new blank page	
Insert a table of two rows and two columns	
2 Observe the Quick Tag Selector	The Quick Tag Selector shows the HTML tree structure for the table.
3 Select the **\<table\>** tag	(From the Quick Tag Selector.)
Click the arrow next to the tag	To display a menu.
Choose **Edit Tag...**	To display the Quick Tag Editor, as shown in Exhibit 7-1. Note that the Edit Tag option is selected.
4 In the Quick Tag Editor, edit the width attribute to **"75%"**, as shown	
Quick Tag Editor — Edit Tag — \<table border="1" width="75%"\>	
	To decrease the width of the table.
Edit the border attribute to **2**	To increase the width of the table border.
Click ✓	To apply the changes.
Deselect the table	The table width is decreased and the table border width is larger.
5 Save the page as **MyTable.htm** and close it	

Topic B: Working in Code view

Explanation   While writing code, it's common to make errors, such as spelling mistakes or typos. FrontPage's IntelliSense feature helps to reduce errors that occur while writing code.

IntelliSense

The IntelliSense feature can help prevent all kinds of common errors, including incorrect tag usage. IntelliSense includes statement completion and displays the parameters available for the code you're writing. It also provides typing aids to speed up the code writing process. The Code View toolbar contains several typing aids that automate tasks, such as inserting comments, applying word wrap, inserting bookmarks, and inserting line numbers.

For example, if you are writing code to insert a table, when you type the letter t, IntelliSense displays a menu in which the table tag appears selected. Pressing Enter replaces the t with the required table tags. Then, pressing Space bar opens a menu that contains parameters, such as border and align, that are available for the table tag. Code IntelliSense is available for HTML, CSS (cascading style sheets), XSL (Extensible Stylesheet Language), JScript, VBScript, JavaScript, and ASP.NET.

Do it!   ## B-1: Using the code IntelliSense feature

Here's how	Here's why
1 Create a new blank page	
2 Save the page as **My page.htm**	(In the current unit folder.)
3 Switch to Code view	
Place the insertion point as shown	``` <body> | </body> ```
Type **<**	To open the Autocomplete menu, as shown.

4 From the menu, choose **h1**, as shown	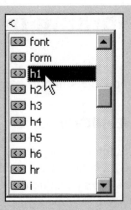
	(You need to scroll down.)
5 Press ⏎ ENTER	The characters h1 are inserted after the < tag.
Type **>**	`<h1></h1>`
	To close the heading tag. The closing tag </h1> appears automatically.

6 Place the insertion point as shown	`<body>`
	`<h1>│</h1>`
	`</body>`

	(If necessary.) You want to add a heading here.
Type **List of Spices**	
7 Place the insertion point after the closing heading tag	`<h1>List of Spices</h1>│`
Type <	To open the Autocomplete menu.
From the menu, double-click **p**	To insert a paragraph tag.
Type **>**	To close the paragraph tag.
8 Place the insertion point after the closing p tag	
Press ⏎ ENTER	
Type **<**	To open the Autocomplete menu.
Choose **h2** and type **>**	To add an h2 heading.
Within the tags, type **Cinnamon**	
9 Switch to Design view	The text you added to the page appears on the screen. The heading 1 style is applied to the first text, and the heading 2 style is applied to the second text.

10 Switch to Code view

11 Place the insertion point after the closing h2 tag

Press ⏎ ENTER

```
<h2>Cinnamon</h2>
|
```

Type **<**

From the Autocomplete menu, choose **font**

Press SPACEBAR   The Autocomplete attribute menu appears.

Choose **color**   You want to define the color attribute of the FONT tag.

Press SPACEBAR

12 Type **=**   Pick Color ...

                                    A small box appears asking you to pick a color.

Double-click as shown   Pick Color ...

                                    To open the More Colors dialog box.

Select a red color

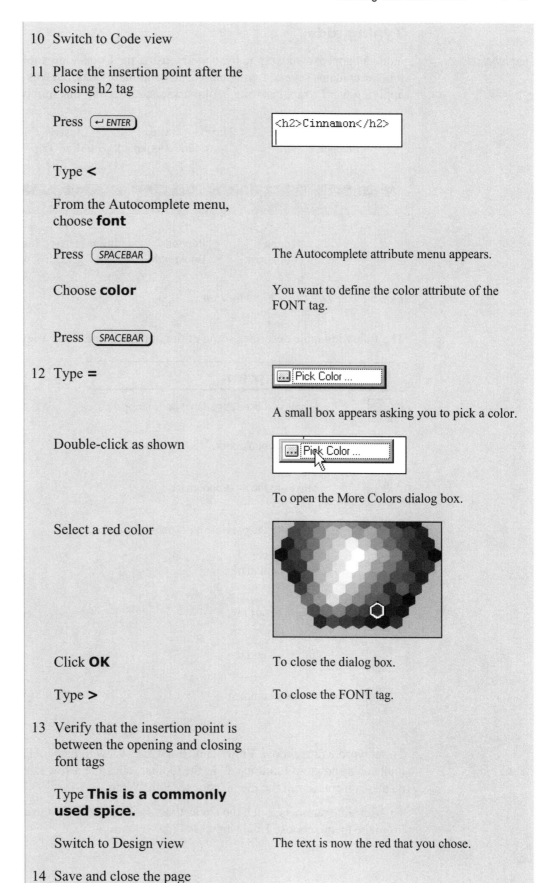

Click **OK**   To close the dialog box.

Type **>**   To close the FONT tag.

13 Verify that the insertion point is between the opening and closing font tags

Type **This is a commonly used spice.**

Switch to Design view   The text is now the red that you chose.

14 Save and close the page

Typing aids

Explanation

You can apply word wrap to the code by using the Code View toolbar. The Code View toolbar contains several typing aids which automate tasks, such as inserting comments, applying word wrap, inserting bookmarks, and inserting line numbers.

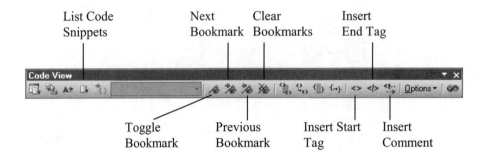

Exhibit 7-2: The Code View toolbar

The following table describes some of the buttons in the Code View toolbar:

Item	Description
	Displays a list of available code snippets.
	Creates a bookmark.
	Moves to the next bookmark.
	Moves to the previous bookmark.
	Clears bookmarks.
	Inserts a start tag.
	Inserts an end tag.
	Inserts a comment.

To set word wrap, choose View, Toolbars, Code View to display the Code View toolbar, as shown in Exhibit 7-2. In the toolbar, click the arrow next to Options to display a menu. From the menu, choose Word Wrap.

To insert line numbers, open the Code View toolbar and click the arrow next to Options. From the menu, choose Line Numbers.

Do it!   ## B-2:   Setting word wrap and line numbers

Here's how	Here's why
1 Open the Products.htm page	
Switch to Code view	
2 Observe the code	The code isn't wrapped. There are long lines of code, and you need to use the horizontal scroll bar to see them.
3 Choose **View**, **Toolbars**, **Code View**	To display the Code View toolbar.
Click as shown	
	To display a menu. Note that the Line Numbers and Auto Indent options are already selected. Selecting the Line Numbers option inserts line numbers in the code, and selecting the Auto Indent option indents code lines in the default style.
4 From the menu, choose **Word Wrap**	To apply word wrap to the code.
5 Observe the code	The code is now wrapped. You don't need to use the horizontal scroll bar to see long lines of code.
6 Click the arrow next to Options	
From the menu, choose **Line Numbers**	To remove line numbers from the code.
7 Save and close the page	

Code indentation

By default, the code generated by FrontPage is indented with default styles. You increase the default indentation of a specific code line to make it more prominent. You can also increase indentation for the tags that you add under a parent tag. For example, the TR tag comes under the parent tag TABLE. So, when you add the TR tag, you can increase the indentation of that line, as shown in Exhibit 7-3. This helps to identify parent-child relationships visually within the code.

```
<table border="1" width="100%">
    <tr></tr>
</table>
```

Exhibit 7-3: An example of code indentation

To modify the indentation of a code line, place the insertion point at the start of the code line. Then, choose Edit, Code View, Increase Indent or Decrease Indent, as needed.

Do it!   **B-3:   Modifying code indentation**

Here's how	Here's why
1 Open My page.htm	
| 2  Place the insertion point after the opening body tag, as shown | ```
<body>
<h1>List of Spices</h1>
``` |
Press (↵ ENTER)	
Choose **Table**, **Insert**, **Table**	
Specify 2 rows and 2 columns and click **OK**	To insert a table of two rows and two columns.
| Observe the code | ```
<body>
<table border="1" width="100%">
    <tr>
        <td> </td>
        <td> </td>
    </tr>
    <tr>
        <td> </td>
        <td> </td>
    </tr>
</table>
``` |
| | Note that the TR tags are indented compared to the TABLE tag. This is the default indentation of code. |
| 3  Place the insertion point as shown | ```
<p></p>
<h2>Cinnamon</h2>
<font color =#FF0000
</body>
``` |
| 4 Choose **Edit**, **Code View**, **Increase Indent** | The code line shifts to the right. |
| 5 Save and close the page | |
```

Finding matching tags and braces

Explanation

When you're dealing with several lines of code, it's often hard to find the start and end tags quickly. For example, if your Web page contains nested tables, finding matching `</TR>` tags can be difficult. The Find Matching Tag option helps you navigate your code and find what you're looking for.

To find a matching tag, select the tag and choose Edit, Code View, Find Matching Tag. The corresponding matching tag is selected.

You might want to find a matching brace when you use scripts in your code. To find a matching brace, select the brace and choose Edit, Code View, Find Matching Brace.

Do it!

B-4: Finding matching tags

Here's how	Here's why
1 Open Locations.htm	
2 In the Code View toolbar, click Options and select **Line Numbers**	To display line numbers with the code.
Identify the table tags in the code	
Select the **<tr>** tag, as shown	```
28 <table border="0px" cellpadd
29   <tr>
30   <td width="672px" height
31
32   <table border="0px"
33   <tr>
34   <td width="113px"
   height="15px"></td>
35
36   </tr>
37   </table>
38
39   </td>
40   </tr>
41 </table>
```
(This TR tag is in line 29.) |
| 3 Choose **Edit, Code View, Find Matching Tag** | ```
28 <table border="0px" cellpaddin
29   <tr>
30     <td width="672px" height=".
31       <div align="left">
32         <table border="0px" ce.
33           <tr>
34             <td width="113px">
   height="15px"></td>
35
36           </tr>
37         </table>
38       </div>
39     </td>
40   </tr>
41 </table>
```
The </tr> tag is selected. Note that there are other TR tags, but only the matching tag of the tag you selected is selected. |
| 4 Close the page | |

Comments

Explanation

Every programming language has its own style for inserting comments within code. *Comments* contain a description about a particular code line or code block. In HTML, comments are inserted inside the comment tags. The starting comment tag is `<!--` and closing tag is `-->`. Any text added inside the comment tags isn't executed, nor is it visible on the Web page. Comments are intended for you, the developer, and other developers who might need to edit the code.

Commenting your code helps you to understand each section of code when you need to update it in the future. It also helps other developers understand what each section is for. You can use comments to indicate any variety of useful information, such as the last modified date, the author of the code, or specific instructions for other developers.

To insert comments, place the insertion point where you want to insert a comment and then choose Code View, Insert Comment. A line with the comment tag is inserted. Then, enter your comment text.

You can also use the Code View toolbar to insert a comment. To do so, place the insertion point where you want to insert a comment, and click the Insert Comment button.

Do it!

B-5: Inserting comments

Here's how	Here's why
1 Open My page.htm	

2 Place the insertion point as shown	`18 </table>`
	`19 <h1>List of Spices</h1>`
	`20 <p></p>`
	
	You want to insert a comment here.

3 Choose **Edit**, **Code View**, **Insert Comment**	`List of Spices</h1><!-- | -->` Note that start and end comment tags are inserted in the code.
4 Type **Main Heading**	The comment is inserted in the code.
5 Switch to Design view	The comment isn't visible. Comments aren't displayed in a browser.
6 Save and close the page	

Bookmarks

Explanation

You create bookmarks in the code to navigate to different code blocks. For example, if your Web page contains several tables, you can create bookmarks at the beginning of each of these tables.

To create a bookmark, place the insertion point where you want to create the bookmark and click the Toggle Bookmark button.

After you create bookmarks, you can move from one bookmark to another easily by clicking the navigation buttons available on the Code View toolbar. To go to the next bookmark, click the Next Bookmark button on the Code View toolbar. To go to the Previous bookmark, click the Previous Bookmark button on the toolbar.

Do it!

B-6:   Creating bookmarks

Here's how	Here's why
1 Open AboutUs.htm Switch to Code view	
2 Place the insertion point before the opening body tag, as shown	`15 |<body topmargin="0px" leftmargin="0px">` `16 |`
3 Click [button]	(The Toggle Bookmark button is on the Code View toolbar.) To create a bookmark. A blue-colored box appears to the left of the line number.
4 Place the insertion point on line 60 and click **Toggle Bookmark**	To create a bookmark on line 60.
Repeat this step on line 100	To create a bookmark on line 100.
5 Place the insertion point near the first bookmark	Click anywhere in line 15.
Click [button]	To move to the next bookmark.
Click [button]	To move to the next bookmark.
Click [button]	To move to the previous bookmark.
6 Click [button]	To remove all bookmarks on the page.
7 Save and close the page	

Code snippets

Explanation

Code snippets are blocks of code that you use frequently. If you know you're going to re-use a section of code, you can set it as a snippet. When you need the code in that snippet, you can simply select the name you gave to your snippet from the code snippet list, and all that snippet code is inserted at your insertion point. This can go a long way toward reducing the time it takes to write code, and it prevents repetitive and tedious code tasks.

To create a code snippet:

1   On the Code View toolbar, click the List Code Snippets button to display a list.

2   In the list, double-click Customize list to open the Page Options dialog box. The Code Snippets tab is activated.

3   Click Add to open the Add Code Snippet dialog box.

4   In the Keyword box, enter a name for your code snippet.

5   In the Description box, enter the description.

6   In the Text box, enter the code and click OK.

7   Click OK again.

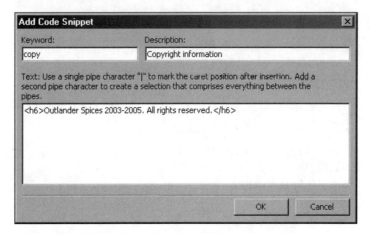

Exhibit 7-4: The Add Code Snippet dialog box

Do it!   **B-7:   Creating and inserting code snippets**

Here's how	Here's why
1 Open Recipes.htm	
2 Click [icon]	

dt2	HTML 2.0 DOCTYPE
dt3	HTML 3.2 DOCTYPE
dt4	HTML 4.01 DOCTYPE
linkrels	LINKREL="StyleSheet"
metad	META Description
metakey	META Keywords

(Customize list...)

	(The List Code Snippets is on the Code View toolbar.) A list appears that contains available code snippets.
Double-click **Customize list**	To open the Page Options dialog box.
3 Verify that the Code Snippets tab is active	
Click **Add**	To open the Add Code Snippet dialog box.
4 In the Keyword box, enter **copy**	Copy is the keyword for this code snippet.
5 In the Description box, enter **Copyright information**	
In the Text box, enter **<h6>Outlander Spices 2003-2005. All rights reserved.</h6>**	(As shown in Exhibit 7-4.) This is the copyright statement for the Outlander Web site.
6 Click **OK**	To close the Add Code Snippet dialog box.
Click **OK**	To close the Page Options dialog box.

7 Place the insertion point at line 508, as shown	`507  <td width="780px">`
	`508`
	`509    </td>`

8 Click [icon]	The code snippets list now contains the newly added code snippet.
From the list, double-click **copy**	The code snippet is inserted in the code.
9 Save the page	
10 Switch to Design view	The copyright line is inserted in the page.
11 Close the page	

Optimizing HTML

Explanation

When you're ready to publish your Web pages, you should consider optimizing your code first. Optimizing your code strips out unused space in each HTML file. This extra space is made up of things like comments, excessive white space, and redundant tags. Getting rid of these things reduces the file size of your Web pages, making them faster to download. You can automate this task by using the Optimize HTML option in the Tools menu.

To optimize your HTML, choose Tools, Optimize HTML to open the Optimize HTML dialog box, as shown in Exhibit 7-5. Select the desired options, and click OK.

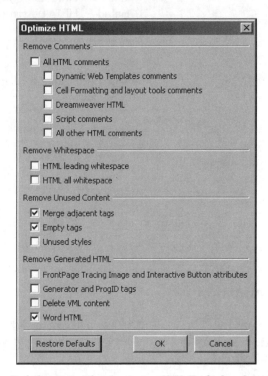

Exhibit 7-5: The Optimize HTML dialog box

Do it!   **B-8:   Optimizing HTML code**

Here's how	Here's why
1 Open Locations.htm	
2 Switch to Code view	To prepare to remove all comments in this Web page.
Identify the comments in the page	(There is only one comment, at line 7.)
3 Choose **Tools**, **Optimize HTML...**	To open the Optimize HTML dialog box.
4 Under Remove Comments, check **All other HTML comments**	To remove the HTML comment in the Web page.
Click **OK**	The HTML comment is removed.
5 Save and close the page	
Close the Web site	

Unit summary: Working with HTML code

Topic A   In this unit, you learned how to view the **HTML tree** structure. You learned how to select and change properties of items in Design view by using the **Quick Tag Selector**. You also learned how to edit tags by using the **Quick Tag Editor**.

Topic B   Finally, you learned how to use the **IntelliSense** feature while writing code. You learned to use the typing aids in the Code View toolbar to set **word wrap** and **line numbers**. You also learned how to find **matching tags**. Then, you learned how to **insert comments and bookmarks** in Code view by using the Code View toolbar. You also learned how to create and insert **code snippets**. In addition, you learned how to **optimize** your HTML code.

Independent practice activity

1 Create a new blank page.

2 Save the page as **My custom page.htm** in the current unit folder.

3 In Design view, insert a table of two rows and two columns.

4 Change the width of the table to **50** by editing the tag properties. (Hint: Use the Quick Tag Editor.)

5 Remove line numbers from the code. (Hint: Use the Code View toolbar.)

6 At the beginning of the table tag, insert a comment that reads **Two by two table**.

7 Optimize the HTML code by removing the comments and all white space.

8 Close the Code View toolbar and hide the Quick Tag Selector.

9 Save and close the page.

Review questions

1 Which feature shows the HTML tree structure and enables you to select and modify HTML tags in Design view?

2 Which feature can be used to create and edit HTML tags within Design view?

3 What are some reasons for adding comments to your Web page?

4 How do you modify code indentation?

5 What are the HTML tags that are used for comments?

6 Which of the following features can be used to prevent repetitive and tedious code-writing tasks by inserting frequently used code?

   A Code snippet

   B Code block

   C Bookmarks

   D Comments

7 When you use the Tools, Optimize HTML command, what is stripped out of the code?

Unit 8

Publishing and security

Unit time: 40 minutes

Complete this unit, and you'll know how to:

A Publish a Web site on the World Wide Web, on LANs, and on the SharePoint Portal Server.

B Set permissions for a Web site.

Topic A: Publishing a Web site

Explanation

When you're finished building your Web site, you need to publish it on the Internet, so that users can access it from anywhere in the world. *Publishing* a Web site simply means copying your Web site to a Web server.

Publishing on the World Wide Web

To publish a Web site on the World Wide Web (WWW), you need an Internet Service Provider (ISP). ISPs provide you with a domain name and a server. A *Domain name* is the name that identifies your Web site on the World Wide Web. For example, www.outlanderspices.com is the domain name that identifies the Outlander Spices Web site on the World Wide Web. You publish your pages to a Web server, which handles permissions, executes programs, and communicates with client computers that make requests to the server.

Network publishing

To share your Web site with others in your organization, you can publish it on a local network, which is often called an intranet or local area network (LAN). An intranet is a private network that allows authorized users in an organization to collaborate in a variety of ways. Typically, companies use intranets to share digital resources, manage schedules and projects, create employee forums, and publish company policies and important announcements.

To make your Web site available to other computers on an intranet, you need to install Internet Information Server (IIS). You might need to consult your system administrator for more help. After installing IIS, you can publish your Web site on the Web server on your machine.

After you publish a Web site on an intranet, anyone connected to the network can access your Web site by typing the network ID of your machine into the browser's Address bar.

You can also use IIS as a platform to test how your Web site looks and functions before actually publishing it to the Web. Then you can publish the Web site from your local server to the server provided by your ISP.

IIS

IIS allows you to use your local computer as a Web server. If you have installed IIS on your machine, you can publish your Web site as a single unit on IIS and check its functionality. You can also set permissions and properties for your Web sites to determine access limits for different users.

IIS also supports complex interactive technologies, such as Common Gateway Interface (CGI) and Active Server Pages (ASP).

Publishing Web sites to multiple locations

You can publish Web sites to different locations, such as local-to-remote, remote-to-local, or remote-to-remote servers. For example, you might want to publish a Web site that you've created to the local intranet, as well as to a Web server on the Internet. You can also publish a Web site to a location on your local computer.

You can publish your FrontPage Web sites on the Internet to an HTTP server, a Web server, or an FTP server. To publish to an HTTP server, your Internet Service Provider (ISP) should have the Microsoft FrontPage Server Extensions or SharePoint team services installed. You can also publish your Web site to the SharePoint Portal Server, if it's installed on your machine or if you're connected to it.

After you've published a Web site, you can publish the same Web site to a different location. To do this, follow the same steps and specify the new destination or the new server name.

Do it!

A-1: Discussing Web servers

Questions and answers

1 You have created a Web site. Before publishing it on the Internet, you want to check if the Web site is working properly. What can you do?

2 Can you publish a Web site to the Internet after you've published it to a local network?

3 What are the common types of servers to which you can publish your Web site?

4 How can you make your local computer act as a Web Server?

5 After you publish a FrontPage Web site to your local computer, you want to publish it to an HTTP server provided by your ISP. What do you need to do this?

Remote Web Site view

Explanation

You can use the Remote Web Site view to publish a Web site to any of the following locations:

- **FrontPage** or **SharePoint Services.** A Remote Web server that supports FrontPage Server Extensions or SharePoint Services.
- **WebDAV.** A Remote Web server that supports Distributed Authoring and Versioning (DAV).
- **FTP.** A remote Web server that supports File Transfer Protocol.
- **File System.** An option that uses a folder on your local computer or on the network as the Remote Web Site.

To publish a Web site, choose File, Publish Site to open the Remote Web Site Properties dialog box, as shown in Exhibit 8-1. By default, the Remote Web Site tab is activated. Under Remote Web server type, you can select any of the four server types. In the Remote Web site location box, enter the location where you want to publish the Web site or click Browse to find the location, and click OK. Then, click Publish Web site.

The location could be your machine name or the server name provided by your ISP. You can preview the published Web site by clicking either the View your Remote Web site link or the Open your Remote Web site in FrontPage link.

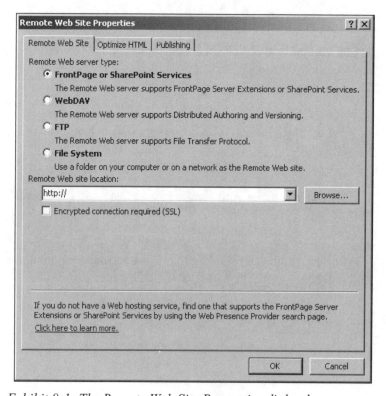

Exhibit 8-1: The Remote Web Site Properties dialog box

Setting publishing options

When you publish a Web site to a server, you can set various publishing options by activating the Publishing tab in the Remote Web Site Properties dialog box, as shown in Exhibit 8-2. You can set options to publish only those pages that have changed since you last published the Web site, or to publish all pages by overwriting the ones that already exist at the destination. You can also set options to determine the changes that have been made since you last published the Web site, either by comparing the source and destination Web sites or by using timestamps on the source files. It is also possible to set options to log changes during publishing. You can later view these log files to see the changes. *Log files* contain information about the changes made in the Web site, such as who made the changes, when they took place, and which pages were modified.

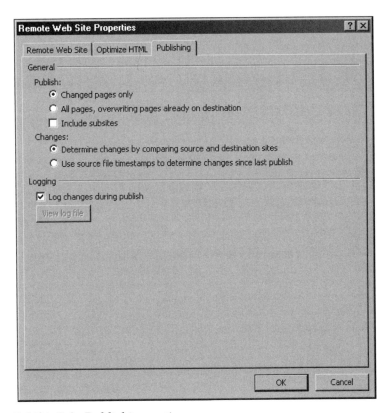

Exhibit 8-2: Publishing options

To set the publishing options, click the Publishing tab in the Remote Web Site Properties dialog box. Then, select the relevant option. If you want to create log files, check the Log changes during publish checkbox, and Click OK.

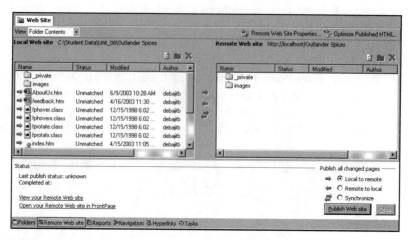

Exhibit 8-3: The Web site after step 4

Do it!

A-2: Publishing a Web site

Here's how	Here's why
1 Open the Outlander Spices Web site	(From the current unit folder.)
2 Choose **File**, **Publish Site...**	To open the Remote Web Site Properties dialog box. By default, the Remote Web Site tab is active.
3 Under Remote Web server type, verify that FrontPage or SharePoint Services is selected	To prepare to publish the Web site on the local machine.
4 In the Remote Web site location box, enter	(The instructor will provide the name of a Web Server to you. In class you will use your computer's name as the server name.) Here, http is the protocol used to transfer the files on WWW followed by the name of the Web server.
http://<server name>/Outlander Spices	
Click **OK**	A message box appears stating that a Web site does not exist at the specified location and that FrontPage can create the Web site.
Click **Yes**	The Web site opens in Remote Web Site view, and it contains two panes, as shown in Exhibit 8-3. The left pane shows the local site, and the right pane shows the remote site.
5 Click **Publish Web site**	(In the lower portion of the Remote Web site view, below Status, a progress bar appears.)
6 Under Status, click **View your Remote Web site**	Status Last publish status: successful Completed at: 6/15/2003 3:09:40 PM View your publish log file View your Remote Web site Open your Remote Web site in FrontPage
	The home page of the Web site appears in the Internet Explorer window.
Close Internet Explorer	

SharePoint Portal Server

Explanation

You can use Microsoft SharePoint Portal Server to create Web portals. *Web portals* are Web sites that offer various services, such as e-mail, a search engine, online shopping, and forums. You can establish a central point of access to all your key business information and applications by using SharePoint Portal Server. You can also share information across file servers, databases, public folders, Internet sites, and SharePoint Team Services-based Web sites.

If your local computer has the SharePoint Portal Server installed, then even the Web sites that you publish to your local computer act as functional Web sites. The *SharePoint Portal Server* is a set of programs extending the functionality of a Web server to your local computer. It's possible to publish your Web site from your local computer to the SharePoint Portal Server, even if your computer doesn't have SharePoint Portal Server. You can do this by connecting your machine to one that has SharePoint Portal Server installed.

To publish a Web site to the SharePoint Portal Server:

1 Chose File, Publish Site to open the Remote Web Site Properties dialog box.
2 Under Remote Web server type, select FrontPage or SharePoint Services.
3 In the Remote Web site location box, enter the address of the SharePoint Portal Server.
4 Click OK.
5 When the Web site opens in Remote Web site view, click Publish Web site.

Do it!

A-3: Discussing SharePoint Portal Server

Questions and answers
1 What is a SharePoint Portal Server?
2 What is the procedure to publish a Web site to the SharePoint Portal Server?
3 If your local computer doesn't have SharePoint Portal Server, can you publish your Web site from your local computer to the SharePoint Portal Server?

Topic B: Managing Web security

Explanation

The security of a Web site is always important, especially if that Web site contains information related to financial transactions or proprietary and copyrighted information. To administer and manage a Web site securely, you can set access permissions. Setting access permissions helps to prevent unauthorized users from accessing the Web site.

Web security

The security of the Web site depends on your Web server and its operating system. FrontPage provides various levels of security that you can assign to users. The following permission options are available:

- **Browse.** This option provides read-only access. Users have permission only to read pages in the Web site. They cannot modify them.

- **Author and browse.** Users can create and modify the content in the Web site, but they cannot add or delete a Web site. They also have browsing permission.

- **Administer, author, and browse.** This option provides full access. Users can add and delete Web sites and set Web permissions and configurations. They also have author and browse permissions.

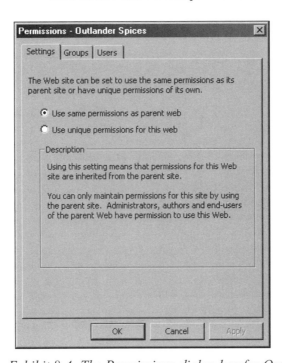

Exhibit 8-4: The Permissions dialog box for Outlander Spices

Setting permissions

To set permissions, you need to open the Permissions dialog box, which consists of three tabs. By default, the Setting tab is activated. On this tab, you can specify if you want to set unique permissions for the Web site. On the Groups tab, you can manage user groups and their permissions. You can also add new groups. The Users tab is used to see the names and access permissions of the current users of the system. You can also add new users on it.

To set permissions for a Web site:

1 Open the server-based Web in FrontPage

2 Choose Tools, Server, Permissions to open the Permissions dialog box, as shown in Exhibit 8-4.

3 Select Use unique permissions for this web and click Apply.

4 Click the Groups tab to add groups of users and assign them rights to browse, author and browse, or administer, author, and browse the Web.

5 Click the Users tab to add individual users and assign appropriate rights to them.

6 Click OK.

7 Click OK again.

Do it!   **B-1:   Setting permissions**

Here's how	**Here's why**
1 Under status, click **Open your Remote Web site in FrontPage**	Status Last publish status: successful Completed at: 6/15/2003 3:09:40 PM View your publish log file View your Remote Web site Open your Remote Web site in FrontPage
	To open the published site in FrontPage. The server-based Web site opens in another FrontPage window.
2 Choose **Tools**, **Server**, **Permissions...**	To open the Permissions – Outlander Spices dialog box. By default, Use same permissions as parent web is selected.
3 Select **Use unique permissions for this web**	To set the permissions for this Web site.
Click **Apply**	
4 Click the **Groups** tab	Browse permission is assigned. This is the default setting.
Click **Add**	To open the Add Groups dialog box. Here, you can add groups of users and give them rights to browse, author and browse, or administer, author, and browse the Web.
Click **Cancel**	
5 Click the **Users** tab	
Click **Add**	To open the Add Users dialog box. Here, you can add individual users and assign appropriate rights to them.
Click **Cancel**	
6 Click **Cancel**	To close the Permissions dialog box without changing the permissions for this Web site.
7 Close the server-based Web site	
Close only the active FrontPage window	The original FrontPage window, containing the local version of the Outlander Spices Web site in Remote Web site view, is now accessible.
Close the Web site	

Unit summary: Publishing and security

Topic A   In this unit, you learned how to **publish a Web site**. You learned that you can publish Web sites on **Web servers**, such as **IIS**, by using the **Remote Web Site Properties** dialog box. You also learned how to publish Web sites on **SharePoint Portal Server**.

Topic B   Finally, you learned how to set **permissions** for a Web site. You learned that you can assign three types of permissions to the users of a Web site; **Browse**, **Author and browse**, and **Administer, author, and browse**.

Independent practice activity

1 Open the Practice Outlander Web site.

2 Publish the Web site as **Practice site**.

3 Test the published site in a browser.

4 Close the browser.

5 Close the Web site.

6 Exit FrontPage.

Review questions

1 Which remote Web server that supports Distributed Authoring and Versioning?

   A FTP

   B SharePoint Services

   C WebDAV

   D File system

2 Which tab in the Remote Web Site Properties dialog box is used to view log files?

3 What are the three user permission levels available in FrontPage?

4 Which location uses a folder on your local computer or on the network as the Remote Web Site?

   A FTP

   B FrontPage

   C WebDAV

   D File system

5 What is the procedure for setting permissions for a Web site?

Course summary

This summary contains information to help you bring the course to a successful conclusion. Using this information, you will be able to:

A Use the summary text to reinforce what you've learned in class.

B Determine the next courses in this series (if any), as well as any other resources that might help you continue to learn about FrontPage 2003.

Topic A: Course summary

Use the following summary text to reinforce what you've learned in class.

Unit summaries

Unit 1

In this unit, you explored the **FrontPage environment**. You viewed Web pages in **Hyperlinks view**, the navigation structure in **Navigation view,** and the folder structure in **Folders view**. Then you explored a page by using **Design view**, viewed the HTML code of a page by using **Code view**, and previewed a page as it would appear in a browser by using **Preview**. Finally, you learned how to use Design view and Code view simultaneously in **Split view**.

Unit 2

In this unit, you learned how to create a **one-page Web site** and **add text** to a Web page. You also learned how to **add a new page** and **import** a page into a Web site. Next, you learned how to **format a page, align text**, and **insert a horizontal line**. You also applied various **text styles**. Finally, you learned how to insert **bulleted, numbered, multilevel,** and **definition lists**.

Unit 3

In this unit, you learned how to **create hyperlinks** and **bookmarks.** You also learned how to **link to an external Web site and to** create a **link to an e-mail address**. Next, you learned how to create a **navigation structure** and insert a **navigation bar**. You also learned how to create a **shared border**, a **bar with custom links**, and **page banners**. Finally, you learned how to **update hyperlinks** to reflect changes to file names.

Unit 4

In this unit, you learned how to **insert, edit**, and **align an image** in a page. You also learned how to **format text around an image** and use **images as list bullets**. Next, you learned how to create and modify **photo galleries**. Finally, you learned how to create **image links** and how to create **hotspots** in an image.

Unit 5

In this unit, you learned how to **insert a table** and **add images** to tables. You learned how to **add** and **delete rows** and **columns**. Then you learned how to **insert nested tables** and add **captions** to tables. Finally, you learned how to modify **table** and **cell properties**, and how to use **AutoFormat** to format tables.

Unit 6

In this unit, you learned how to **set page properties**. You learned how to add **rollover effects to a hyperlink**. You also learned how to apply and change a **theme**. Finally, you learned how to **customize a theme**.

Unit 7

In this unit, you learned how to view the **HTML tree** structure. You learned how to **edit tags** by using the **Quick Tag Editor**. Then you learned how to **optimize** HTML code. Next, you learned how to use the code **IntelliSense** feature and set **word wrap** and **line numbers.** You also learned how to find **matching tags** and insert **comments** and **bookmarks**. Finally, you learned how to how to create and insert **code snippets**.

Unit 8

In this unit, you learned how to **publish** a Web site. You also learned how to publish Web sites to the **SharePoint Portal Server**. Then you learned how to **set user permissions** for a Web site.

Topic B: Continued learning after class

It is impossible to learn to use any software effectively in a single day. To get the most out of this class, you should begin working with FrontPage 2003 to perform real tasks as soon as possible. Course Technology also offers resources for continued learning.

Next courses in this series

This is the first course in this series. The next course in this series is:

- *FrontPage 2003: Advanced*

Other resources

You might find some of these other resources useful, as you continue to learn about FrontPage 2003. For more information, visit www.course.com.

- *HTML 4.0: Basic*
- *HTML 4.0: Advanced*

F r o n t P a g e   2 0 0 3 : Basic

Quick reference

Button	Shortcut keys	Function
	CTRL + **N**	Creates a new blank page or displays a list of options
	CTRL + **O**	Opens a Web page or displays a list of options
		Shows or hides the folder list in Page view
		Aligns text or graphics to the center
	CTRL + **S**	Saves a Web page
	F12	Previews the Web page in a browser
		Formats the selected text to a bulleted list
		Formats the selected text to a numbered list
		Increases the indentation of the selected paragraph or text to the next tab stop
	F7	Checks a Web site for spelling errors
	CTRL + **K**	Inserts a hyperlink for the selected text or at the insertion point
		Inserts a picture from a file to the Web page
		Creates a rectangular hotspot
		Creates a polygonal hotspot
		Draws a table in the Web page
		Applies changes in the code

Button	Shortcut keys	Function
		Displays a list of available code snippets
`<>`	CTRL + ,	Inserts a start tag in the code at the insertion point
`</>`	CTRL + .	Inserts an end tag in the code at the insertion point
`<!--  -->`	CTRL + /	Inserts a comment in the code at the insertion point
	CTRL + F2	Creates a bookmark in the code at the insertion point
	F2	Moves to the next bookmark
	SHIFT + F2	Moves to the previous bookmark
		Removes all bookmarks in the page

Glossary

Bookmarks
Used in the code to easily navigate to different code blocks.

Bulleted list
Used to display items of more or less equal importance (also known as *unordered lists*).

Cell
The intersection of a row and a column in a table.

Code snippets
Blocks of code that you use frequently.

Code view
Used to examine and edit the HTML code.

Code view toolbar
Contains buttons for automating tasks, such as inserting comments, applying word wrap, inserting bookmarks, and inserting line numbers.

Comments
A description about a particular code line or code block. Any text added inside the comment tags isn't executed, nor is it visible on the Web page.

Containers
Tags that have a starting and a corresponding ending tag.

Definition list
Used to define terms or to create a list, such as series of items and their descriptions.

Design view
Used to create, edit, or format a page. Editing in Design view is similar to editing a document in a word processor.

Domain name
The name that identifies your Web site on the World Wide Web. For example, www.outlanderspices.com is the domain name that identifies the Outlander Spices Web site.

Empty tags
HTML tags that don't have closing tags.

Ending tag
Identical to the starting tag, except that it contains a forward slash (/) before the tag name, such as </HEAD>.

External links
Hyperlinks that link to other Web sites on the Internet.

Find and Replace
A feature that allows you to find a specific word in a document or throughout a Web site and replace it with another word.

Find Matching Tag
A feature helps you navigate your code and find code that matches the selected item.

Folders view
Used to access and organize the files and folders of a Web site.

FrontPage Editor
Used to view the HTML code and preview a page as it would appear in a browser, both in a single view.

GIF
A common image format that is typically used for logos and image-based text.

Home page
The first page you see when you view a Web site in a browser. It usually provides a welcome message or a statement that describes the purpose of the Web site.

Horizontal line
Used to divide the contents of a page visually into different sections. (Also called a *horizontal rule*.)

Hotspot
An informal name for a link within an image.

Hyperlink
Text or an image that is tagged with a Uniform Resource Locator (URL) that connects Web pages. You can move from one page to another by clicking hyperlinks.

Hyperlinks view
Used to see all the hyperlinks view all the hyperlinks associated with the selected page at a single glance.

Hypertext Markup Language (HTML)
The standard markup language for the Web. It uses a series of predefined tags to define the structure and presentation of a page.

Hypertext rollover effects

Special formatting that can be applied to hypertext links when the user points to the link. This setting is found in the Page Properties dialog box.

HTML tags

Define the structure of a page. Each tag consists of the tag name surrounded by angular brackets, such as <HEAD>.

Image map

An image containing hotspots.

Images folder

Stores the images that you use on the Web site.

IntelliSense

A feature that helps reduce errors that can occur while writing code, such as spelling mistakes and incorrect tag usage.

Internal links

Hyperlinks that link files within a Web site.

Internet

A vast network of countless smaller computer networks located all over the world. It provides the medium for the Web.

Internet Information Services (IIS)

A Web service you can use to create, configure, and manage your Web site.

Internet Service Provider (ISP)

Provide you with a domain name and a server.

Intranet

A private network that allows authorized users in an organization to collaborate in a variety of ways.

JPG

A common image format that is typically used for photographic images that contain many colors.

Level-one heading

The highest-level heading (H1) that's meant to define the top heading structure for a page. The next level headings are named H2 through H6. Each heading level implies a hierarchical structure.

Log files

Contain information about the changes made in the Web site, such as who made the changes, when they took place, and which pages were modified.

Mailto links

Hyperlinks that activate a user's e-mail application and create a new e-mail form set to a specific address (also called *e-mail links*).

Microsoft Office Picture Manager

An extension of Microsoft Office 2003, it's the default image editing application for FrontPage 2003.

Microsoft SharePoint Portal Server

A set of programs extending the functionality of a Web server to your local computer.

Navigation bar

A set of links to various parts of a Web site that appears on most or all of the pages in the Web site.

Navigation structure

Defines the hierarchy of the pages and provides visitors with a simple and consistent way to move around a site.

Navigation view

Used to create and view the navigation structure of your Web site.

Nested list

Used to display data of various levels, as you might see in an outline.

Nested table

A table that's inserted into a cell of another table.

Numbered list

Used to display items in sequence or items of descending importance (also known as *ordered lists*).

Optimize HTML

A tool that strips out unused space in each HTML file and reduces the file size of your Web pages, which makes them faster to download.

Page banners

Images or text that is used to add titles to multiple pages on a Web site. Page banners are created inside a shared border.

Photo gallery

A collection of pictures arranged in a specific layout on a page. You can arrange pictures on one page or across multiple pages, like a photo album.

Picture actions

A button that displays a list of appropriate actions that can be taken for the selected picture.

_Private folder

Stores form results and other files that are hidden from users.

Publishing

Copying your Web site to a Web server so that users can access it from anywhere in the world.

Quick Tag Editor

A feature that helps you create and edit HTML tags within Design view.

Quick Tag Selector

A feature that shows the HTML tree structure and enables you to select and modify HTML tags in Design view.

Shared borders

Areas in the margins that contain the same elements on all the pages in the Web site.

Shortcut menus

Displayed by right-clicking an item, they contain a list of common actions that you can take on the selected item.

Split view

Used to view a page in Design view and Code view at the same time. When you make changes in Design view, you can see the corresponding changes in Code view take place at the same time, and vice versa.

Starting tag

The HTML tag that identifies the information that follows it. Starting tags have a corresponding ending tag.

Table

A grid composed of rows and columns with data contained in individual cells.

Table caption

A title for the table that appears at the top of the table.

Task pane

The FrontPage window element that provides options to perform common tasks. For example, you can use the task pane to search for a file, create a new page, or open a Web site.

Theme

A set of background and foreground images, formats, and font styles that is applied to all the pages on your site or to specific pages that you select.

Uniform Resource Locator (URL)

The address of a document or other resource on the Web. For example, http://www.outlanderspices.com is a URL that represents the address of the Outlander Spices Web site.

Web browser

Software application, such as Internet Explorer and Netscape Navigator, that enables you to navigate within and among Web sites.

Web portals

Web sites that offer various services, such as e-mail, a search engine, online shopping, and forums.

Web site

A collection of hypertext documents (HTML files), graphics, and media files.

World Wide Web

Commonly referred to as the "Web," it's the most popular service of the Internet.

Index

T

V

W

X